CONTENTS

Exercise in Cross Cultural Phenomenology

Dismantling the Hegemony – Calling All Anarchists

February 2009

Are people finally fed up with political authority? Discussions of anarchy seem to be fashionable these days. In some countries people are even taking to the streets. From theocracies like Iran to democracies like Greece, we are witnessing the sights and sounds of nascent insurrections and fledgling revolutions. Ever greater numbers of disenchanted citizens from around the globe are showing the telltale signs of mounting dissatisfaction with political hierarchy – authority founded principally upon power, privilege, and the use of force – whether through taxation, police or military might, economic enslavement, or other means of social control. (More recently, we have seen the toppling of a dictator in Egypt insurrection in Libya, and mounting destabilizing activity throughout the Muslim world).

The fact is there has never been a human social grouping – primal, ancient or modern – that has not relied upon the judgment of its more experienced members. But *institutionalized hierarchical authority*, perched atop a stratified societal structure, only emerged with the birth of cities – with civilization.

Unrestrained license has never existed in any human social grouping for an extended period (with the exception, perhaps, of present day Somalia or Wall Street investment bankers). Yet the example among extant indigenous tribes and bands – and most likely those primal groupings going back two million years throughout the Pleistocene – suggests an *egalitarian* non-hierarchical model based on consanguinity and affinity, and providing us with the best illustration of a functioning anarchic community. In those pre-civilized groups, research strongly suggests that authority was not imposed by some remote and mighty king, magistrate or legislator – elected or otherwise, sitting atop some pyramid of power; rather, guidance was provided through tribal elders related to all members by extended bonds of *kinship* – natural "leaders" who offered direction based upon personal relations, acknowledged wisdom, and proven experience.

If we would call ourselves anarchists, then we must seek to understand the roots of our current predicament – the straitjacket of political power from which we wish to loose ourselves, as well as the world and consciousness that was forsaken when we first donned this constraining garment. To do this, we must explore the foundations of human freedom located in our primal, pre-civilized past. So, in that sense you may call me a primitivist.

The hierarchical structure of modern political institutions must be understood in its origin if we are to find a way of successfully overcoming it. And we must explore the conditions of social life that existed prior to the birth of political hierarchy and social stratification if we are to find an adequate model to replace the systems and institutions by which we now find ourselves encumbered. None of us want a revolution only to replace one system of hierarchy with another regime. But what can the habits and traditions of early, pre-civilized humans tell us about how to live today?

Millennia before arriving on the shores of the New World, our earliest civilized forbearers had already forsaken a more primal self-sufficiency and autonomy for the apparent safety and security afforded by obedience and conformity to emergent hierarchies of political power and social control. America itself now represents the apex in this process, culminating in a modern scientific spirit directed by specialists with an Enlightenment driven pursuit of progress, an unwavering belief in reason, historical causality, and the rule of law.

Anarchy – real critical anarchy – needs to get beneath the gentle surface appearances of our distaste for authority, and understand the feral instincts that fuel our discomfort. Only by thinking and feeling at this primitive, organic level can we begin to dismantle the hegemony and the guiding architecture of those who would control us. But, if we remain trapped in their worldview, we will never find the means to overtake them.

*****

Mothers of Invention

March 2009

It is broadly believed there is an inherent structure to the universe. People take for granted that it is simply a matter for scientists to discover this structure and thereby understand the laws that govern both nature and humankind. However, it is increasingly evident that no such structure exists; that there is no design simply given in nature independent of our perception. And those events or regularities that we might point to as demonstrating some inherent pattern may only be a function of the screens we have chosen to cast over the world in order to fit it into a specific framework, usually in order to manipulate things according to the ends we wish to achieve. Moreover, such "ends" are customarily prefigured in the very frameworks chosen. Even the cosmic regularities – periodicities we might identify in nature – are, in this light, only contingent patterns, resulting from the particular screens that we chose to apply.

The structures thereby established are not really discovered, so much as we create them; and they are variable, changing depending upon the conceptual screens and tools one chooses. This has happened throughout the history of philosophy and science. In fact, the so-called laws of nature that the various sciences have "discovered" have been revised and overturned one century (or one decade) after another with further reflection or refinement by means of applying yet new sets of screens. Furthermore a religious screen will give you a quite different model than a quantum physics screen. And there are any numbers of other screens we have developed and applied as well in the history of culture. We are in fact born into a world of screens that we learn to accept as givens; and if not, we wind up in the rather unenviable position of village idiot, genius, outcast, madman, or witch.

One might argue that our primitive fore bearers, our pre-civilized ancestors, also experienced the natural world through some basic conceptual or symbolic screens as well. Certainly we have what we would call evidence of some rudimentary screens regarding kinship structure, and relations to the natural world. But we cannot reconstitute or experience that world quite as the pre-civilized mind experienced it (see Owen Barfield, *Saving the Appearances: A Study in Idolatry*).

In fact there emerged in the writings of some of the earliest civilizations a new screening tool early on perfected by the Greeks, and recast by legislators, scientists, and other specialists down through the ages - the syllogism. The syllogism, as a screen, itself signaled the rise of modern scientific and historical consciousness, as did none other; and it became embedded as the lynchpin of western rationality. "This is how social laws were made and natural laws were made or 'discovered'" (Bram, *The Recovery of the West*). And yet, even modern physics continues to question and overturn previous screens, and the "laws of nature" that we took for granted just decades ago (see Julian Barbour, *The End of Time: The Next Revolution in Physics*).

One may choose to call our current situation, and the changes it has wrought, "progress;" others may call it unfortunate. Even the concept of progress is part of a larger conceptual screen through which we judge and assign meaning and value to the world around us. It is a concept born at the dawn of history, with the beginnings of specialized realms of knowledge - science, religion, polity, economy, etc.

These diverse screens reveal not matters of fact, but rather, different ways of imposing structure on the given (whatever that is); and such screens can be destructive of the world as given.

But then the question remains, how do we raise and educate our children when we ourselves have forgotten? Do we simply present the world we have structured as absolute fact, and send our youth off to war (or on mission) to convince those non-believers that it is our way or the highway? Or do we acknowledge that the structures we have created, and come to feel comfortable believing-in, are not necessarily the only way of being in the world, and that we may learn from others what we have buried beneath our own taken-for-granted assumptions. It is a personal, social, political and philosophical question.

*****

Who would have thought that before he took office at the top of Obama's to-do list would be fighting pirates and pigs? Well that is the case. Not one hundred days into his fairytale presidency, Barack Obama is dealing with two issues that were not even on the radar screen last fall. But why are pirates and pigs so important, and how did the issues they present, holding sailors and the world's populations hostage, come to occupy center stage in our efficiently run and digitally globalized country? The answers may be simpler and more frightening then we first suspect.

It has been a long time since Captain Hook once sailed the waters off the coast of Neverland. And, the Pirates of the Caribbean? Why, that was just a movie that kept repeating itself. But those young boys in speedboats taking sailors and ships hostage off the coast of Somalia...that is real. And it all began two decades ago as young Somali fishermen no longer had safe and plentiful waters in which to fish for their villages' own survival. Their livelihood had been destroyed. How, you might ask? By the illegal and often clandestine encroachment by fishing fleets from more "developed" nations like South Korea, Japan and Spain, among others. The pillaging of the Somali coastline began shortly after the dismantling of Somalia's last government in the early 90's. A 2006 United Nations report noted that,

> *In the absence of the country's at one time serviceable coastguard, Somali waters have become the site of an international 'free for all,' with fishing fleets from around the world illegally plundering Somali stocks and freezing out the country's own rudimentarily-equipped fishermen.*

And according to another U.N. report, approximately $300 million worth of seafood is stolen from the Somali coastal waters each year. It appears that initially it was these young fishermen who turned to piracy in order to protect their own waters against larger, and more sophisticated trespassers, whose equipment, technology and firepower outpaced the ability of small local Somali fishermen. In addition, several European nations found that it was "more cost effective" to use these same waters as a toxic waste dump for years. And now the bills are becoming due. We more 'developed' nations of the world have created, it seems, the conditions leading to the piracy we are now desperately fighting to control. Our policies and practices, driven by motives of profit and economic expansion, have led to this current crisis.

And now to the pigs! Despite how much we might try, this too is not traceable back to the small farms and underdeveloped village areas of the world, like those in rural Mexico, Thailand or China. No, it is a direct result of large-scale domestication, live stocking and agribusiness farming that has created our current crisis. Again, it is the developed nations and their corporations that have created the dilemma. While in the earlier part of the 20th century most pig farming was conducted by small farmers in backyards and small family plots, agribusiness eventually bought up the smaller players (who could no longer afford to compete) and harvested these farms into large colonies or 'pig cities' of tens of thousands of pigs, with a commensurate increase in the potential for squalor, waste and disease.

Moreover, the IMF and World Bank further complicated the problem by requiring smaller 'developing' countries to open their economies to outside corporations if they wanted IMF loans. So agribusiness moved in and, without the same oversight and regulation, closed down the smaller indigenous players, and created "cities of pigs that stretch around the world," hotbeds of disease. And it is big American-based agribusinesses like Holly Farms, Tyson and Perdue, holding large pig (and poultry: remember the bird flu) farms that are at the center of the latest flu pandemic scare.

Now, what is the common denominator among these pigs and pirates? And why am I forced to view these twin challenges together, as the result of a common cause? Could it have to do with the tendency of modern industrial society towards economic and political expansionism, operating with a competitive, zero sum-game rationale? Could it have to do with the fact that such 'civilized' games necessarily create winners and losers? Perhaps there is just something about the values underlying our civilized societies, with our commitment to hierarchy, divisiveness, and control that mechanically negates those who are different, the strangers, and systemically creates victors and victims, masters and slaves. When will the developed world of 'civilized' nations realize that they have been living in a dream, imagining their own omnipotence, and that now the dream is ending and we must admit finally that we have given birth to a nightmare? But, perhaps the nightmare is only just begun!

*****

May 2009

With America in the lead chariot, Western civilization has engineered a hegemony that is rapidly overtaking the globe – politically, economically, and culturally. This has unleashed a domination of values that, unlike hegemonies of the past, is lightning fast, wide ranging, and spreading insidiously, enabled by those very technologies it has created and which it seeks to market to the world. All the while America has touted its singularity and its greatness, its "manifest destiny," offering refuge – nay, salvation – to all who would learn how to partake of its many benefits, comforts and ideologies. But, is there trouble in paradise?

Let's begin with democracy, American-style. Having been forcibly "peddled" around the globe like miracle snake oil – pushed into the most unlikeliest of places, including the Middle East, Eastern Europe and elsewhere – such "democratization" has provided, ironically, yet greater credence to groups we consider well, how should I say this, non-democratic' – elements like Hamas and Hezbollah. And we have supported questionable leaders who are anything but representatives of democracy, leaders like Saakashvilli in Georgia, Yushchenko in Ukraine, and Karzai in Afghanistan. But, this is really nothing new; we have been propping up political puppets for many decades, just as our political puppets at home are propped up by capital. Oh, but how democracy is a wonderful tool for propagandists!

Capitalism as well has taken wing and exported itself to the farthest reaches of the planet, creating an economic and financial hegemony unparalleled in history, with a preponderance of American cultural artifacts popping up in the oddest of places to prove it. Our cultural seeds have been cast wide upon the waters for all of posterity. So now citizens of every nation on earth may partake of the insidious slavery inherent in the "free" market. It is amazing, however, how the boldest efforts of democratic capitalism have run up against their own worst instincts. It is as if the underbelly of the beast has been laid bare, and it does not look all that attractive from this new vantage point.

Another interesting wrinkle in our current predicament – as

specialization in every profession increases at exponential rates with the advance of scientific and technological knowledge – we are finding in the health care realm alone that we have run into a shortage of primary care physicians here in the land of plenty. Why this dilemma? Because in the greatest, richest and most advanced (read: specialized) country in the world, doctors want to be specialists as well, in order to benefit from the additional prestige and money that goes along with that specialization. Otherwise they just appear to be another part of the expanding, or is it shrinking, proletariat.

And as the great moral fiber of our country seems now to be proliferating cases of schoolyard bullying, mass murder and extreme cases of domestic and random homicide on our streets, we ask why. Yet we never want to acknowledge that our own society, our culture and our politics have advanced bullying and aggressiveness as the keys to success in both business and international affairs. And, lately we have even resorted to the worst kind of bullying behavior, including torture and the murder of innocents (Iraq, Afghanistan) at every turn; just look at our performance on the world stage over the past several decades.

Finally, Lou Dobbs and other minor pundits engaged in their own bullying techniques, began whining on cable TV years ago about how most middle class Americans were being cut out of the American Dream, loudly demanding that home ownership and access to other middle class perks be made more easily available to the common citizen. Now we find that this whining and bullying reached the financial markets and federal regulators and has helped precipitate a housing bubble and crash the likes of which has never been seen before, and a financial crisis of global proportions as Americans one-and-all reached out for the golden rings passed out by lenders who were only too pleased to give in to the bullying and look the other way as they collected their ill-gotten revenues, spinning them out into credit default swaps. Indeed, the bullying began with the pundits and talk show hosts, and trickled down to the legislators, regulators, mortgage brokers and banks, and the greed was all too willing to step up to the plate. Like a disease, it spread quickly, until the poor populace was well housed and fed. Now the chickens have come home to roost; and we are looking for the greedy bullies to punish; but they are US.

Perhaps Obama can change our ways, lower our expectations about lifestyle, transform our self-perception and our perception of the natural world, reduce our dependency on oil, provide universal health care to all Americans; well these are some interesting daydreams. But, just maybe it is not the problem of American exceptionalism per se.

Perhaps American exceptionalism itself is rooted in a much broader challenge, rooted somewhere at the beginnings of Western civilization, close to the alluvial banks of the once "fertile" Fertile Crescent, at the intersection of the Tigris and Euphrates Rivers in, of all places, Iraq. I say it again; have the chickens come home to roost? Would not that be poetic justice! Is our hegemony, tracing its own manifest destiny back, just the culmination of an historical process that began millennia ago, a process that perhaps cannot be undone by simple political maneuvering or other commercial chicanery – like getting the people to just go out and spend more money or vote?

*****

June 2009

It is no surprise how the usual suspects keep regurgitating the same old myths about implementing a public option for the healthcare coverage in America.

What are these myth-makers (business and politically conservative elements) kidding us about; our access to healthcare services under the current insurance and other managed-care options is already restricted. Unless you have the 'Cadillac' of insurance programs, and pay the substantial premiums that go along with it, your access to healthcare is already rationed, and closely managed.

Who among us can just walk into a specialist these days, without first getting permission from our primary care provider (PCP)? And then, when the PCP finally looks you over and tells you how everything seems fine... "Just take some more cough syrup and go home"...but leave your $20 co-pay on the way out first.

And if you do get the chance to see the specialist, you are lucky if insurance covers the visit; and god-forbid if that specialist suggests further tests, higher-priced drugs or surgery. Now the care-manager assigned to your case from the insurance company begins to monitor your care, and moderate between you and your provider - reviewing your charts, history, and determining the limits of the company's liability for covered services. Remember, these folks are motivated by maximizing profits and, thus, reducing operating costs. So you are at the mercy of the typical short-term thinking and corporate greed that goes into managing for quarterly or monthly performance.

Myth two. The government option will drive the other commercial insurers out of business. Hardly! Big yawn! Those buyers who are well paid and well heeled will always opt for the more expensive plan. There may be fewer insurers in the market, with smaller ones falling by the wayside. And cost competition should bring some of the profitability margins down with the bigger ones. But, a government option will not lead to the annihilation of commercial options. Especially in the USA, there are just too many rich-folk who will always pay for the expensive alternative, whether or not the service is significantly better.

The final myth is that the delivery of healthcare services will deteriorate across the board, especially in the public-option. But, the logic does not follow. The taxpayer finances the public-option; and so the focus would seem to be on servicing those who are 'capitalizing' the venture (the taxpayers), and not lining the pockets of corporate managers or profit-hungry capitalist investors.

*****

The Fertile Crescent and the Dialectics of Freedom

June 2009

Well, there you have it! Once again we find ourselves at the origins, where industrial-strength politics and religion both got their start, back to the birthplace of Western civilization - home to ancient Mesopotamia, Babylonia, Assyria and Persia... or modern day Iran.

From the bosom of these ancient empires emerged an overpowering combination of ruling elites, theocratic and political, who laid the disparate foundations for civilized authority ever since. And, now we see these hegemons playing out their hands in full Kodachrome color, surreptitiously displayed before our eyes on virtual communities and social networking portals born in the West, and exported far and wide – portals that themselves have forcefully subverted the authoritarian control attempted by Iranian theocratic and political establishments.

Of course we are shocked, horrified and excited by such scenes of emergent revolutionary chaos; but grateful that this exercise in apparent democratic rebellion is having a chance to let its images be seen around the world. And, why are we all so engrossed?

Of course, we are rooting for the human spirit to overcome the hegemonic power of its overlord. And we yearn for all people to experience freedom from the slavery represented by such repressive regimes. And certainly, we think of what it would mean if the threat of a nuclear Iran could be erased within a few weeks or months, if the protests are successful.

But, it may also be the case that we fear for our own covert enslavement to the selfsame systems of political and religious authority - systems we both love and hate, and continuously fight to moderate. (I suggest one spend time looking at Jeff Sharlet's book, *The Family: The Secret Fundamentalism at the Heart of American Power*.) And why are we upset in America that our fearless leader (Barack Obama) is treading so tenderly on the issue of interfering in the Iranian demonstrations? Do we want to be seen as more assertive, more controlling, more manipulative, like our distant cousins - the Iranian hegemons? Perhaps, we ourselves distrust our own assumptions of freedom. Maybe we even long (unconsciously) for more overt control in our own society - be it in the form of nationalized healthcare, financial regulation, government ownership of production, homeland security, etc.

And who are those arguing for greater US intervention in the Iranian situation, the same anointed among us who brought us the Patriot Act, Homeland Security, domestic wiretapping, those who fought for the initial invasion of Afghanistan and then Iraq, who sang to us about 'bombing Iran,' who suggested banning books from the Anchorage public library, and even now champion the right of domestic militiamen to bear arms (even semi-automatic weapons) against their fellow countrymen and women here in the USA. There appears historically, existentially, to be some moral equivalency between religious extremism and fanatic politics in any statist context, whether in a Machiavelli, a Stalin, the Supreme Leader of Iran, Ahmadinejad, Saddam Hussein, our own outspoken domestic defenders of torture, or vice presidential candidates who are religiously driven to vilify their opposition even to the incitement of domestic terror. In all there seems to be a sense of moral righteousness, of moral indignation, motivating the fanatic to act on their beliefs.

And have we not already intervened forcefully enough in the current strife in Iran? After all, it is our 'new media' technologies, born in the USA, that have given voice and color to the Iranian people's struggle. No matter what we think, our influence is felt around the globe, almost without pause these days. This is the benefit, the legacy, and the challenge of our own hegemonic role in world affairs. The question remains: who is controlling whom?

I do not seek to justify the Persian-Iranian regime, nor defend our own President's cautiousness abroad or aggressiveness at home. I am trying to sort through the complex relations that both repel us and attract us to the events now unfolding – globally and domestically – and our own awkward ambivalence about 'involvement'. I am raising the question about the relationship between freedom and authority, and the proper exercise of power (political or religious) in a 'civilized' nation. Have we not seen the dragon's head of our own religious conservatives this last election, raising the specter of a new era in theocratic rule right here in the land of the free?

*****

Field of Dreams

July 2009

Not too long ago we Americans became quite certain that our way of life represented the shining star of civilized progress, the very summit in scientific, technological and moral advancement. What we as a nation had achieved, so we thought, was a dream come true. And it is this American Dream that we have held out to (or perhaps aggressively thrust upon) the rest of the world as the true meaning of the "good life" –- the proper goal or end of human existence.

After all, it was our economics, our politics, our science and technology that conceived and fleshed-out this dream world to begin with... a world of personal automobiles in every garage, single family homes with private fenced yards, lawn-mowers and well designed and manicured suburbs, credit cards on demand, all the latest modern conveniences, electronic gadgets and games galore for children and adults alike.

So now that the world is facing multiple crises of staggering proportions - environmentally, ecologically, financially, economically, politically, psychologically and spiritually - where does one lay the blame? Where do we look to better understand the roots of such crises? While pursuit of the American Dream may be initially fingered as a proximate cause of our crises, we were not alone in our reliance upon certain fundamental assumptions and values that made it all possible. Practically all civilized regimes, from ancient Mesopotamia to modern China, can share in the blame since all share some basic assumptions about the pursuit and exercise of power – the necessity for nation building, organizing for war, directing cultural progress, structuring and regulating economic activity.

Barack Obama's recent comments in the Russian capital during a two-day summit with President Medvedev and Prime Minister Putin only serve confirm the above contention. Speaking to graduates of the New Economic School in Moscow, he stated, "The pursuit of power is no longer a zero-sum game... Progress must be shared." To clarify, the real issue is not whether the pursuit of power is a zero sum game; but simply, that it is a game invented by civilized nations for ensuring their (global) influence and driving progress. The real import of his remark was in acknowledging pursuit of power as a cornerstone of nation building, and that the progress of a nation or regime is effected through the exercise, consolidation and enhancement of economic and political influence or control.

Expanding the hegemonic power of America and its dream required not just ingenuity, but lots of industrial energy and productivity, a good deal of land-clearing, substantial pollution, gross dissipation of natural resources, incredible amounts of human labor, trillions upon trillions of dollars in public and private financing, political wrangling and a good deal of social engineering and international exploitation. In short, the American Dream not only set a new standard for what civilized people expected from life, but it also laid the foundation for massive exploitation and abuse - of ourselves, our fellow humans, and our planet... a direct consequence of trying to manufacture, market and live The Dream. And yet, while we were destroying our planet in this quest, have we really made our personal lives better, more enriched, more satisfying and fulfilling?

Well, of course, the skeptical reader might proclaim, "America has the highest standard of living in the world, and we are an example to the rest of humanity... we are 'that shining city on a hill' that Ronald Reagan spoke about. And we have achieved this status because America is the land of the free - the hope of the world!" Since our founding this has been our national calling card. And the beacon of lady liberty at the entrance to the New York harbor has been a symbol of that freedom and that dream around the world.

'Give me your tired, your poor, yearning to be free...'   *Your huddled masses*

But what exactly have we come to understand by this word "freedom"? What does it mean to American's today? And how has this quest for freedom realized itself in terms of America's lifestyle and living the American Dream?

Maybe it is free time that we have in such abundance here in America! That must be it! Well, come to think of it, this doesn't appear to be the case since we seem to work almost 24/7 - more than any other people on the face of the earth. We are slaves to the time clock, the electronic calendar, the blackberry and any other number of mobile devices marketed for our (read: society's) benefit. With all of this focus on the business of work and schedules, there appears to be very little free time to call our own. True, this compulsion - this apparent slavery to the clock - has made us the most productive and efficient people on earth. But this very "efficiency implies the reification of time... a preoccupation with past and future." So where is there any opportunity for the fleeting present - for freedom from the clock - in which to enjoy the good life and the fruits of our labors?

Along with squandered planetary resources, the fleeting reality of the present moment has all but vanished from American consciousness and from Western experience in general. Many of us seem to live in a perpetual state of anticipation - waiting for our next promotion, a pink slip, or that vacation, a new car, getting the kids through college, retirement, or just waiting for our scientists and politicians (our specialists) to find solutions to our latest round of crises.

If one looks even cursorily at life in America today, and the direction of technological innovation supporting and directing our life ways, it becomes clear that freedom for the American psyche is not freedom to live in the present; rather, with respect to time, we are and remain slaves of the future and the past. We seem, rather, to be more concerned with freedom of movement, of place and location. But, trains, planes and automobiles have given way to wireless networks, mobile devices and virtual communities.

Our search for freedom, beginning with our ancestors' move across the Atlantic from the Old World to the New, has led us to erect a world where we no longer need to be tied to any one place, no longer dependent upon a particular location or home; we are free to roam without anchor, without encumbrance, but also without real kinship or community. And to keep in touch with other freely floating, almost disembodied, newly minted "friends" and family we have virtual networks that give us the illusion of being connected and being stable. But this is a false sense of connection, and a false stability - part of the illusion spun by our engineers and marketers - but it seems to provide a feeling of freedom that many of us have now come to pursue and enjoy today.

But is it really freedom of mobility that we so cherish and believe we have achieved, or is it yet another, more compelling sense of freedom that haunts us? Is it perhaps freedom from personal identity, an attempt to escape our own embodiment, an almost pathological yearning for anonymity in an increasingly anonymous world that globalized, urban environments and virtual networks provide us with, so that we can be anyone we want to be or no one at all? Is it perhaps a desire to escape our own flesh, our very selfhood? Is the anonymity of wireless, urban virtuality merely a way of escaping that objectified sense of self, which reified linear historical time has created for us? Interestingly enough, it appears that the anonymity of the Internet and its social networking has provided us with a way to *make believe* we are who we want to be; to be more, better, or other than who or what we actually are; maybe that is the freedom we covet.

The truth of the matter, however, may be quite the opposite. The disembodied virtuality of a wireless and networked world may only provide one with the illusion of anonymity and the promise of an unidentifiable freedom to be. In fact, it may instead lead to a real loss of freedom, to greater public identifiability, and the possibility of being singled out in a wholly networked and connected global village. In this event, not only does it make us slaves to the new media, but it also increases our vulnerability to the state, the perennial political and social forces of manipulation, monitoring and control. Where then is our freedom, and what then of our dream?

*****

Victims of the American Dream

August 2009

We Americans have been spoiled: our desires, wholly unrealistic. It is a disease that has become epidemic. We should wake up and see how the rest of the world lives. Not only are we coddled; in spite of this wealth it seems that increasingly we have become a nation of self-proclaimed victims – a phenomenon that has led others around the world to see us as just a bunch of whiners.

A few years ago, I had caught bits of a cable news program

demonstrating the telltale signs of this growing American malady. Commentator Lou Dobbs was hosting another of his televised series of town halls to incite the masses, lamenting the fact that the American Dream was no longer available to a majority of our middle-class citizens.

Well, what did he expect? Must every citizen's dream come true? Does Lou Dobbs want a government guarantee? Do we need a government take-over? Wasn't that the old Soviet model? Even if this American Dream is achievable, and if there is sufficient equality of opportunity in the USA to pursue it, does everyone have the right to expect fulfillment of his or her dreams?

I recently read that the American Dream is a myth overdue for revision. Maybe so; or perhaps this dream has always been just that – a dream. And it will continue to remain so for many Americans simply because this dream, or myth, is not static but an ever-changing goal painted by expert marketing professionals who encourage us to want and expect more than we can ever afford. Then just at the moment when we believe we have arrived at the horizon of our dream, the marketers move the goal farther away from us. Everything is a commodity, and unsatisfied consumption is the name of the game.

The great majority of our citizens have only been able to participate, albeit marginally, in this dream by living on debt. This is no dream; it is more like a nightmare, with debt as far as the eye can see – mortgages, credit cards, insurance premiums, taxes, defaults, lawsuits, and bankruptcies. What other dreams can this great country devise for its citizens? How much longer can the evanescent promise of "cowboy capitalism" persist, until finally collapsing in upon itself? It seemed to me that Dobbs' program was nothing more than our national cult of victimization now running at a fevered pitch, stirring an already boiling pot of chronic American disenchantment. And leading, in the end, to global financial collapse.

Had not America originally been populated by boatloads of disenchanted immigrant forbearers who, out of frustration over their own victimization, set sail for the New World with the intention of ending their persecution and rectifying the wrongs that had been inflicted upon them by older religious and political hierarchies. Lest we forget the words etched on Lady Liberty, the idol of the new motherland:

Give me your tired, your poor,   *Your*
huddled masses yearning to be free,   *The*
wretched refuse of your teeming shore.   *Send*
these, the homeless, tempest-tossed to me...

So America became the land of victims, those seeking refuge, and later of quick fixes for all those who felt victimized still. Did not these very same victims, seeking a new life in the New World then turn right around and inflict the same or worse injustices, victimizing others right here in their "New Jerusalem?" Think of the American Indian, those "savages;" think of the settlers' own puritanical women-folk, those "witches." Perhaps there is something about the values underlying our civilized society, with its commitment to hierarchy, divisiveness, and control that mechanically suspects those who are different, the strangers, and systemically creates victors and victims, masters and slaves.

Is it possible we have all becomes slaves, victimized by the very Dream that promised to set us free?

*****

September 2009

We Americans are slowly but unmistakably coming to the unsettling realization that our hegemony keeps seeking its own expansion and empowerment, whether one party is running it or the other. In the end it is all a matter of power, its accumulation and consolidation. And no matter what Obama said in Moscow earlier this summer about the acquisition of power no longer being a zero sum game, he was just smirking at Putin and us through his pretty teeth.

Refusing to acknowledge that he had made a cooperative accommodation on missile defense shields in Poland to demonstrate a sharing of power with the Russian Federation, he and his surrogates offered some sophomoric comments about "bad intelligence" on Iran and some vague sentiments about doing what is "best for our national interests." Not that I am for more defense spending in Eastern Europe or anywhere else for that matter, of course not. But the least Obama could have done is publicly acknowledge that an important reason for his decision not to pursue Bush's missile defense strategy was because he understands that we live in a multipolar world, and that he (and the USA) cannot continue to act like an implacable imperialist hegemon. Yet, he refused to admit such.

And now Obama wants to prove to us domestically, once again, that power is not to be shared, but hoarded and abused... and that ours is not a government of, by, and for the people. Rather, this is a government of the powerful against the peons. He is now asking Congress to renew the Bush-Cheney policy embedded in the "Patriot Act" that will continue the use of numerous questionable domestic surveillance techniques on American citizens, whether or not there is real justification for such snooping.

This same hegemony is also going to demand that you and I (and all Americans) are vaccinated for the swine flu or risk being jailed - I mean "quarantined" - for our refusal; all for the good of the country, of course. And further, if he gets his way under the proposed legislation, we will all be required by law to purchase health insurance or be fined for our decision not to. God is this a great country, or what? ...Land of the free, home of the brave!! Is that psycho-talk, or what?

And now we hear further that the *hegemon* is telling us that the free flow of information on the web is bad for us and bad for democracy. Yet, he certainly did not find fault with it during his election cycle run-up. He seems to use whatever tactics and approaches suit his drive to enlarge and consolidate power... Nietzsche called it, the Will to Power!!

As we recently read in The Hill's Blog Briefing Room:

Obama said that good journalism is 'critical to the health of our democracy,' but expressed concern toward growing trends in reporting -- especially on political blogs, from which a groundswell of support for his campaign emerged during the presidential election... 'I am concerned that if the direction of the news is all blogosphere, all opinions, with no serious fact-checking, no serious attempts to put stories in context, that what you will end up getting is people shouting at each other across the void but not a lot of mutual understanding,' he said.

I guess it won't be long now before Obama does what the Iranian Theocracy did last summer in the wake of fallout from their fake elections... outlaw the blogosphere and silence those who don't comply! No folks, it is not a zero-sum game anymore... it is now a negative sum game! Let the games begin!

*****

October 2009

Have you ever been lulled into compliance by the Siren's sweet voice like Ulysses was, or seduced by the charms of a ravishing temptress? Perhaps you have felt the rapture of transcendence brought on by listening to 14th century Gregorian chants.

Well, just like the ritual seductiveness of religion and the regimented requirement of work, online social networking lulls us into a placid acceptance of the necessity of civilization and its artifices - those carefully constructed distractions that keep us harmlessly in line like domesticated cattle, so that we accept the outcomes of its political machinations as necessary evils.

President Obama and his cronies are expanding a machine that is well oiled and, for generations, has been primed to release toxins that will continue to decimate the people of this nation. And healthcare 'reform' is only the latest example of the disease that is spreading. The healthcare 'debate' in the US Congress is just the most recent symptom of the illegitimacy of politics in America, revealing the true nature of this 'kabuki' theatre called democracy, our servitude to the State, and the meaninglessness of the institutions of government – democratic or otherwise.

The healthcare tax provision is real my friends (either by forced premiums or by fines), and it will soon become the law of the land. We will no longer complain about a death tax in our country, for we will have a Life Tax as well. If you are alive in America you must pay, whether or not you work, eat, or drive. As long as you are breathing you must pay! You have no rights in this country, no freedoms... only duties and obligations!! And this illusion of our freedom is further exposed by the light of day.

... It's bad enough that the [Max] Baucus bill says 'the consequence for not maintaining [health] insurance would be an excise tax' and the House bill requires a 'tax on individuals without acceptable health care coverage....' Now Senator Olympia Snowe is reiterating the position that 13% of income is an acceptable maximum out-of-pocket cost for health premiums. That is

financially devastating for families at 400% - 700% of the Federal Poverty Level (and many at higher levels). Since the President has ceded extraordinary power to her, this is likely to become law if she so chooses. It's a windfall to the insurers and a body blow to working Americans. [From the Huffington Post]

And where is the political activism, the conscience in this country? Where is the outrage, the rebellion? Where are the people calling its government to task for its continued exercise of raw power? It is gone; the will to resist has been dissipated by the distractions and toys of a civilization that would crumble if people could only find their instinct to challenge it. And social media, the newest toy in the arsenal of civilization, is only the latest of distractions; and it distracts surreptitiously, while providing the illusion of engagement, of resistance, of revolt.

Facebook and Twitter create apathy, not action. They are just additional tools of civilization's ruling elite, to keep us under the thumb of their political hegemony. We remain enslaved to these distractions, which keep us from taking responsibility for our lives - going where we need to go and doing what we need to do. It is like an elixir, a drug, used by the ruling hegemony to keep us enslaved to them and their 'system' forever!

In fact, we do not just accept such obedience; we applaud it, sanctify it, celebrate it and encourage it -- in our selves and our fellow 'citizens'. It is a sad time for us, as 'we the people', as humanity sinks deeper into a quagmire of its own making.

Whether it is peaceful assembly in Pittsburgh, H1N1 vaccination refusals in New York, healthcare debate in Washington, US action in Afghanistan, or even election protests in Iran... the battles are already lost. In brief, we have all abdicated our primal autonomy, together with the sanctity of kinship and clan, and the guidance of those who would know us and love us. And we have abdicated such for the feigned comfort of being directed, controlled, imprisoned, enslaved and tortured by the chains of our own acquiescence to political power. Enjoy your freedom people, as the red carpet is rolled out.

*****

A certain pathos has become the crippling disease of the soul of western civilization. Particularly in America, a deep sadness haunts our obsessive pursuit of individual excellence – the lone ranger embarked on the solitary and strenuous path of achievement – leading to the slow but certain destruction of real autonomy and vital consanguinity, as the final bell tolls for the imminent demise of family, kin, and community. And what are the symptoms of this disease?

Having fought so hard to realize our ill-defined and poorly considered quest for individuality at all costs, we have inadvertently (or perhaps intentionally) created virtual 'communities,' disembodied worlds that enable us to remain unfettered and unscathed by the fleshiness of personal contact and the intimacy of real relationships. The physical world gone, we now sit self-directed and self-enclosed, safeguarding our lunacy, our anonymity, our unspoken weaknesses and our unsightly blemishes. Safely they remain tucked away in our tweets and our twitters. Our longing has created its perfect match; a pathetic, substitute world in which we call unseen strangers friends and collect electronic followers to "tweet" while we engage in highly cultivated and dissembling displays of honesty and self-disclosure.

I will say again, what I've voiced elsewhere:

[These] global villages... are erector set villages, artfully crafted from our own infantile dreams... They claim to "connect us." But, it is a hollow promise aimed at disarming a potential epidemic of cultural alienation that might otherwise expose the tinkerers on the scaffolding propping up the gloss of our blueprinted lives.

And all of this activity is generated with the sole purpose (often unbeknownst to us) of giving our lives a sense of importance, of sharing, of community, of the relationality that is genuinely missing from our real everyday experience. We have achieved the ultimate in self-possessed independence, so much so that we now yearn unconsciously for the 'connectedness' that we worked so diligently to free ourselves of in the first instance.

We share the trivialities of our daily goings-on, our clumsy missteps, and our secret privacies with those who would be watching us – our friends or followers. We are all voyeurs and exhibitionists seeking the thrill of connectivity without the weighty consequences of real live community or sensuous commitment.

We are pathetic in our desperate outreach, our selfish grasping for attention, for recognition, for acceptance ("I have more friends/followers than you!"). And yet, at the same time these "tweets" have their nerve, the gall to speak about the lack of human communication in the world they inhabit daily. Imagine, they cannot communicate with others in that real world, so they cobble together a world of interlocutors to complain about the lack of real communication in their hum-drum lives. And all of this tinkering is aimed at the dispensation of folk wisdom and other idiocies -- miniature homilies condensed into 140 or 240 characters. We are bombarded with so many proverbs and anecdotes about correct behavior, achieving success, and being happy; about how to communicate online and how to get more followers; as well as loftier topics like love, the good, the right, the true, the beautiful and, of course, the Tao. And they all welcome one another with good morning wishes and good night kisses.

Then again, perhaps this betrays a deeper pathos, our discomfort with the natural silence that surrounds us. And so, rather than abide such silence, we prefer to fill it up with any noise just to hide our distress. And while it may provide us with an illusion of meaningful discourse, and the vague comfort of fitting-in, it really does nothing of the kind. In fact, such "communication" becomes a malicious sham to keep us from focusing on our own disaffection and loneliness so that we fail to appreciate the pleasure of silence in recovering ourselves from this culturally-imposed estrangement, and hearkening again to that authentic, faintly, wild voice within.

Finally, all of these friends and followers of ours have very clever names or descriptions of themselves: "philosopher on the loose," "geniusartistic," "biomodern magician," "intuitioneer," "discerner of archetypes," "racialicious," "americansatori," "cardiotonic psychedelia." Oh! You who believe you are free and freely associating as you please. You are just following the protocols of those manufacturers of post-modern experience who pull the strings and make you dance. Truly we have become hollow men. All I have to say is good night tweets – sleep tight.

*****

The Future of Humankind

December 2009

Many people in the developed world speak today about envisioning a real, sustainable, post-industrial future. Like them, I too would welcome conditions of greater reciprocity among peoples and with the earth. A post-industrial culture certainly sounds intriguing, but it seems somewhat difficult to imagine what it would be like given the history of culture in civil society and its transformative impact upon everything from human consciousness to global ecology.

Certainly, it is not impossible to visualize a world with electric cars, wind farms, and less-destructive, more earth-friendly agricultural methods. It may even be possible to dream of a world with little, if any, nuclear threats and fewer wars. However, even these alterations in behavior will require a deeper transformation of human self-understanding and of our place in the world.

As a species, we have made a series of perhaps unalterable choices beginning approximately 6,000 years ago with the birth of urban life – civilization – the effects of which have positioned us as we now find ourselves in the world. These choices have molded our expectations and requirements about what life should be like - in short, the purpose or ends towards which we feel human life and culture should be directed.

This overarching vision with all of its unquestioned assumptions has crystallized itself in the now-taken-for-granted concept of "American exceptionalism" – our self-proclaimed political, economic, and moral superiority, and the apparent hegemony of our cultural values. This belief and its underlying values have been cast around the globe like gasoline before a wildfire, as we have pursued a scorched earth policy of global domination through cultural transformation/occupation. Some groups, nation-states and countries find these values desirable, others abhorrent. Some try to mold themselves to the vision enunciated by such expectations, while others arm themselves to the teeth to fight-off the insidious occupiers.

Having planted our flag at the summit of western civilization and declared our own "manifest destiny," we Americans continue to believe that we have set the right example for mankind to follow, and that we are justified leading the rest of the human race to fulfill its proper role in our civilization. We set ourselves up long ago as protectors of moral virtue, cultural innovation, political institution, economic progress, and human rights. And much of the western world has followed our lead in this myopic belief, unchallenged until very recently.

Do not misunderstand me; we have indeed achieved a great deal, especially in terms of medical, information, and other advanced technologies. But at what price; can our unflinching drive for innovation and progress, for complete dominion over the uncertainties of our natural environment and animal natures — a drive that began ages ago with specialization, spurred on by investment capital and individual risk taking, motivated by the acquisition of private property and wealth – can this rocket ship of science and technology, fueled by the resources of capitalistic expansion, be brought to a stop; can it be slowed down, can we alter or reverse its trajectory?

I believe the answer to this question is not simply an economic or even a political one; and this is because the question that it begs is deeply philosophical. Can human consciousness and human self-understanding be redirected significantly enough to alter the social, political and economic trajectory of modern society? That is the more fundamental question. But, if we seek an affirmative answer to this question; then further questions must be asked of modern man, if the future is to be transformed in the manner we might envision.

Can we reintegrate the nuclear and the extended family within the framework of a worldview that is overtly driven by radical individualism? Can we rebuild social networks based upon consanguine and affine relations, rather than upon the authoritarian forces of an anonymous political power elite, whether elected or otherwise?

Can we learn to live without the expectation of high-speed worldwide travel on demand, and instead be more content to live a peaceful life in proximity to where we were born, with those we know and love close by?

Can we restructure our spatial expectations about towns, villages and communities so that we do not need individual transportation vehicles (cars) just to live normal everyday lives? Can we ever become comfortable again with the idea of walking places, or using reliable public transportation when necessary?

Can we adjust our expectations about money, wealth and comfort, and be content to live more simply, more modestly on the earth? Can we adjust how we understand work, and learn to accept less productivity, perhaps zero economic growth, and begin to enjoy life more on a daily and hourly basis? And, can those countries that are finally beginning to taste the apple of American capitalism that has been shoved down their throats be convinced that it was all a mistake, and that tasting this will really be the root of their destruction?

Can we learn to sing and dance, and to feel our bodies again, without shame or embarrassment? Can we stop "tweeting" for virtual friends, while demanding ever-new gadgets and technologies of our technical masters, and ourselves and just be content with fewer prosthetic parts, and try not to be superheroes?

Can we be honest with ourselves and with one another that we have in fact been arrogant and divisive, and not just American's with their exceptionalism, but all who partake in the special traditions of our civilization, past and present, that have culminated in this unique story that we call human history?

Can we step back enough to reclaim a more natural place within the animal kingdom, and recover from our early civilized need to dominate nature, and the substantial hangover that really came in to its own with Francis Bacon and the scientific method, and our transition into the modern era of infinite progress?

These are some of the hard questions that must be asked. The answers are still uncertain, as we seek to simplify our own lives and our households, to better reflect the realities we find immanent and already beginning to impinge upon us.

*****

Tinkerers on the Scaffolding

February 2010

The tame and domesticated contours of civilized life have eclipsed the feral core of everyday experience – that irrepressible anchor of human embodiment, our elemental interlacing with nature, "that subtle knot which makes us man." Neglecting this wild core, we've relinquished our original gift of freedom, the inherent power of just being-there, outside the chains of time and the terror of history. Forsaking this primal autonomy, the groundwork was laid for our own entrapment, the beginning of our enslavement.

Ever since discovery of the appearance of Homo habilis approximately two million years ago, humankind has been defined as toolmaker, technician, and tinkerer. Whether or not a direct link to Homo sapiens can ever be definitively unearthed is a moot point. Clearly we humans live and die by our tools. But, while necessity may be the "mother of invention," what manner of need could have led to the never-ending flow of new tools and technologies evidenced today? What of this unyielding pace of technological innovation that seems to be of another, qualitatively different order?

The Greek "techne" suggests "craft" or "art," the practical discipline of making things. Technology, then, would refer to the results or products of techne – artifacts, devices, tools, and other handicrafts – the artifices of human culture. This sounds like an old story, about which we can be neutral. But we are not neutral; we adore our modern technologies excessively. Is it because they create nice, clean, artificial surfaces, insulating us from the wild and uncultivated underbelly of life, of nature, of our own embodiment?

With America leading the way, the path charted and engineered by Western civilization has spawned a hegemony that is rapidly overtaking the globe, socially, economically, and culturally. This unheralded ascendancy has unleashed a domination of values, which unlike political hegemonies of the past, is lightning fast, wide ranging, and spreading insidiously, artfully enabled by those very technologies to which it has given birth.

Engineering and technological sophistication now appear to constitute the religion of a new epoch. The foundation stones of a nascent techno-theocracy, they march us, hyper-rationally, to a contrived and perhaps apocalyptic Eschaton. Their dominion is so complete that they have undermined our very enjoyment of a more spontaneous life, lived naturally on Mother Earth. After all, the "virtual reality" they promise seems less messy than the real thing.

With an implacable call for progress in our visually dominated world, it is no wonder we are so enthralled by the steady array of new toys and tools paraded before our eyes. But why do HDTVs, TiVos, iPhones, iPods, cell phones, Blackberries, electronic notebooks, and a myriad of other digital gadgets hold such sway, and command our rapt attention? Some might call it convenience; others would say it's just the fulfillment of the American Dream – the Holy Grail of our continuously advancing civilization.

A large part of this digital delight may simply be a function of its visual appeal, the marketing hook that drives our consumerism. Perhaps it really is all about the spectacle. Or maybe it's the continuous enhancement in microchip effectiveness and processing speed, betraying our "end user" mentality – to accomplish more things more quickly so we can buy more toys and move more rapidly into a brighter future.

More pointedly, perhaps, these technologies serve as valuable tools of social, economic, and cultural control. They encourage and validate our fixation with civilization's fundamental construct, unilinear time and its underlying implication – the necessity of historical progress. This insures our continued dependency and our unquestioned faith in a certain path or trajectory, let us call it the curriculum of the West.

All the while, these same technologies distract attention from the inchoate, but developing sense of our own anonymity in today's digitized, urban landscape. They signal the arrival of a new world, the global village, where we all share common values and concerns. But it is an erector set village, artfully crafted from our own infantile dreams of omnipotence – Western domination – now exported around the globe. These technologies claim to "connect us."   But, it is a hollow promise aimed at disarming a potential epidemic of cultural alienation that might otherwise expose the tinkerers on the scaffolding propping up the gloss of our blueprinted lives.

So our suspicions go undetected and our faith in the curriculum remains intact. We continue on, accepting as axiomatic that the paths of technological advancement, happiness, and righteousness coincide; in fact, we take for granted that progress is a good in itself – the only legitimate means of achieving happiness and living the good life. But why can't we jettison this belief? Why this insatiable need for novelty? Why is it we have so little regard for what is primal and founding? And, why do we attempt to light up every corner of the globe, demystify the naturally chiaroscuro quality of life, making everything one-dimensionally bright?   What is it about the curriculum of the West that is so captivating?

It may be that this race for technological innovation is nothing other than the best efforts of our civilization to ensure that we citizens keep producing and consuming, and remain focused on the future. We are being led to the abattoir of our own planned obsolescence by a marketing wizardry that locks us firmly onto a path of never-ending progress. Could this also explain our disproportionate emphasis on free will and unrestrained choice in America? After all, it provides an unassailable platform from which to produce and market an inexhaustible stream of saleable products and commodities that in turn validates our freedom, again keeping us future-oriented and chasing the ever-receding horizon of our Dream.

Who can argue with the shrewdness of such an agenda, or its efficacy in herding us into quiet submission? I was just as susceptible, just as committed to the plan, as were my fellow citizens. But I also sensed that this driving "will" to consume was not part of my natural constitution. It seemed to be the result of a story we had all been told about the future, about "making something of ourselves" and "getting ahead."

Certainly, no one can deny that America has achieved global distinction along with a corresponding smug vanity for its material advancement and its extravagant pursuit of innovation. Nor do I wish to underestimate the value of specific advances in medical science and biotechnology. But that does not mean all progress is necessarily good, or even necessary.

Can I let go of my MacBook or do without email? No. Not completely. But, I refuse to buy the iPhone, the TiVo, or the Kindle; and I reject a host of other gadgets and toys presented to me as necessities. I know that I am being pursued, ensnared in a vicious cycle of work-buy-owe, and that I was partly to blame for the entire arrangement. I was a willing accomplice, collaborating with our clever cultural missionaries. I had become just another spokesperson trying to sell the Dream to the rest of the world, perpetuating the illusion.

Yet, along with most of my fellow citizens, I could not just renounce all the prosthetics provided me without some consequences. The social covenant our ancestors had entered into long ago guaranteed that each and every one of us would come to rely on these tools as a matter of simple survival. I recalled what Rousseau, perhaps the single most important Enlightenment figure, had written centuries before in his work, On the Social Contract:

[Civil society] must transform each individual into a part of a larger whole ... deny man his own [natural] forces in order to give him forces that are

alien to him and that he cannot make use of without the help of others.

As I now see things, we have proceeded too far down this road for anyone to turn back. If anyone is to survive in civil society before its demise – and really, one can no longer leave it completely because our own natural forces have long ago been replaced by civilized ones over generations of indoctrination to the curriculum – then we have little choice but to make use of the tools provided in the interim. So, like many others, I am in a double bind from which I cannot easily escape. But at least I now understand the game, the rules, and the potential consequences of playing it. With this awareness I can develop a healthier positioning with respect to the curriculum and its artifice; I no longer permit its insidious and unchecked control over my life.

Face it! It is far too late to save anything; and *Gaia* does not need saving in any event. The earth, along with civilized greed, will just have to deliver the final blow to our vanity. But in the aftermath we might again awaken to that sense of primitive sovereignty, and relearn to experience the untamed, ecstatic undercurrent of life.

*****

Fascism of the Literati: A Closer Reading of Chris Hedges

April 2010

A modern apologist for the current Western-scientific hegemony, Chris Hedges fails to see beyond the prism of his own totalizing hyper-rational lenses. He is quick to point out the "fascism" inhering in the agenda of the Radical Christian Right or a similar Ur-fascism in atheists like Christopher Hitchens and Sam Harris. Yet, he refuses to question his own scientific fundamentalism and its fascist tendencies.

His own post-enlightenment scientific worldview is propped up on a foundation much like those he warns us against – a cult of White European masculinity, the apocalyptic violence of war, a civilizing "purification" of the natural world through manipulation and domestication, i.e., destruction of ecosystems and species, ushering in a utopia of well-manicured landscapes and machine-tooled citizens. And this hegemony wants to be master of the universe more stridently than any of the followers of Allah, Falwell or Hitchens, imposing its authoritarian, militaristic iron fist on the entire planet.

In fact, the scientific worldview that informs Mr. Hedges' argument is more fascistic in its imperializing tendencies than either the radical Muslims or the fundamentalist-Dominionist Christians and new atheists he criticizes. Mr. Hedges' assumptions about "human nature" and the evil of the human heart are themselves dogmatic and totalizing. And the consequences of such beliefs are clearly and uncompromisingly carried out by the hegemony of Western civilization, forcing its own worldview, morality and economics down the throats of every living creature, if not purifying, than at least seeking to subdue the beast of that (imagined) evil human nature. Welcome home, Thomas Hobbes.

At base, the hyper-rationality that underlies and motivates his critique is every bit a secular religion, on his own definition; and it propounds the use of violence as a cleansing agent with the goal of continual moral, material, and economic progress... these are foundation stones animating his own political worldview, no less than those he criticizes.... rife with the same bigotry, racism, and binary, us-them mentality, that he calls to task.

This Western hegemony has used violence against nature, and against thousands of different cultures, in the name of scientific, technological, economic, and moral progress. But whose progress is this? And why must the rest of the planet be made to suffer under its yoke? This fascism seeks to control, clean and sanitize every corner of this globe so that it can all look and operate just like it does underneath the umbrella of post-modern Western imperialism, destroying anything that stands in its way.

But, as well, Mr. Hedges wants to criticize science and reason when used as a stick by those new atheists like Mr. Hitchens. Yet he fails to see the applicability of this critique to his own hyper-rational ideology. For example, he criticizes the Dominionists for their support of teaching creationism in the schools, on the grounds that it has no scientific validity; teaching creationism, he says, is an attempt to "destroy the possibility for dispassionate, honest, intellectual, and scientific inquiry; it is to make facts interchangeable with opinion, to make lies true..." it is a war against truth, "seeing the world around you through a distorted, ideological prism."* On the other hand, he criticizes Mr. Hitchens precisely for using Western rationality in the service of his atheism. Sorry, but you cannot have it both ways, Mr. Hedges. Yet, he ignores the contradiction. His ignorance is certainly understandable, if not offensive. For he too has been brought up on the *curriculum of the West*, and cannot see clearly due to the profound influences it has had on his own psyche.

It is too bad that Mr. Hedges cannot see past the images of his own distorted and totalizing prism. His modern scientific, hyper-rational worldview is fraught with more ideological assumptions than the rest of those he criticizes combined.

[*In video interviews on the CBC, The Hour, regarding his two books with, *American Fascists* and *I Don't Believe in Atheists*.]

*****

Human reason so delights in constructions, that it has several times built up a tower, and then razed it to examine the nature of the foundation. It is never too late to become wise; but if the change comes too late, there is always more difficulty in starting a reform. The question whether a science be possible, presupposes a doubt as to its actuality. But such a doubt offends the men whose whole possessions consist of this supposed jewel; hence he who raises the doubt must expect opposition from all sides. [Kant, Prolegomena to any Future Metaphysics]

We are told that history begins in Sumer, near the Persian Gulf, where the first civil laws were instituted roughly fifty-five hundred years ago. Coincident with this founding, there emerged entirely new ways of thinking, acting, and interacting with one's fellow citizens. With those first social laws, citizenship was born. The overwhelming evidence from anthropology, archeology, paleontology, ethnography and the history of religions strongly reinforces the view that a new set of problems arose with the transition from an egalitarian kinship-based, predominantly nomadic hunting/gathering lifestyle characterizing the Paleolithic, and autonomous villages representative of the Neolithic, to more sedentary, hierarchically structured life ways, based primarily on intensive plant and animal domestication economies, that erupted onto the scene at the close of the Neolithic period.

This transformation had an incalculable impact upon human consciousness over the ensuing centuries, producing entirely novel categories for understanding and manipulating the world. Reality was constituted differently after the birth of civilization than it had been previously. This would have resounding reverberations for all generations to follow, entrenched as they now were in new hierarchies and institutions that would appear — including formal institutions of education. Borrowing terminology, I will call this new model according to which reality was thereafter constituted, the *curriculum of the West*. The burgeoning temperament for this new way of seeing the world affected every dimension of life as civilization spread, and cities continued to populate the globe over subsequent millennia.

Along with the shift from communal sharing of essential resources, to privatization of access to those resources, a cardinal issue to surface from this change of perspective was the need for control: control of the natural world to ensure food supplies, and control of the citizenry to ensure the protection and safety of those supplies.

With respect to control of nature, scientific inquiry eventually found its voice, leading to the articulation of laws by means of which nature could be manipulated. The first formal laws, following an explicitly scientific logistic, appeared in Greece only about twenty-five hundred years ago; but their foundations were laid much earlier - their necessity issuing from the demands of a sedentary lifestyle and early proto-scientific pursuits to gain control over the agricultural cycle.

Second, with the fracturing of kinship in now stratified social settings of kingdoms, cities, and satellite villages, the need for control over persons also became paramount. This was particularly true in larger urban centers, whose populations were comprised mainly of displaced villagers and other relocated strangers. In this context, revealed religion often aligned with already entrenched political hierarchies - temple and palace together - served to provide sacred law for the conduct of individual behavior and control of social relations, religious ritual itself serving a proto-political function.

Other emerging disciplines soon set about constructing alternative ways to dissect or cut up the world, identifying effects and linking them to causes on a newly established unidirectional temporal axis - an historical timeline. Through the proper application of the new logistic - linking universals to particulars in the form of laws - prediction and control were achieved. Scientific laws of course would give predictive control over nature; religious laws, control over human affairs. And history would become a story of the adventures of these diverse but interlaced controlling hierarchies - religious, political, and scientific.

Seemingly locked in eternal strife, science (with its "discovered" laws) and religion (with its "revealed" laws) would be enemies in posture only - mutually dependent sibling rivals, established at the dawn of civilization, providing guidance and control in hierarchical institutions now dominating modern life. The conceptual foci of these two siblings - the empirical and the transcendental - were simply two sides of the same advancing historical consciousness, reflected as well in the pre-Socratic philosophical struggles over "being" and "becoming." Quite simply, science and religion staked out two complementary positions on one and the same "objective" reality appearing in the breach from prehistory to history.

In addition to the problem of control, however, there also arose the question of meaning, of history's purpose. If we citizens were now locked in a unidirectional historical trajectory, with a present moment that was simply waiting between an historical past bearing down on us and an anticipated future pulling us forward, then what was the purpose, the goal, the endpoint of this forward movement?

Scientific rationality certainly provided the scaffolding upon which to build civilization's "tower" but could give no clear guidance about the ultimate purpose of historical life, or insight into the meaningful "end" of history. Religion, on the other hand, offered a vision of the ultimate goal, the telos of history, but needed science to supply it with a fallen world of mere objects, along with the unfolding historical drama against which the transcendental vision could play itself out. Together they succeeded in focusing human intuition and praxis on what appeared to be the appropriate direction of historical consciousness - the future, progress, and achieving the proper "ends" of life.

It seems almost axiomatic today that progress has become a good in itself - some might even argue the only legitimate means of achieving "the good life." Indeed, scientific rationality and engineering prowess now appear to constitute the new faith of a new era. The foundation stones of a nascent techno-theocracy, they may be marching us, hyper-rationally, to a fabricated and perhaps apocalyptic Eschaton. Their dominion is so totalizing they have undermined the simple enjoyment of a more spontaneous life, lived more simply on mother earth.

In addition to a foundation razing critique of the curriculum, we are in desperate need today of a vocabulary and a path that allows for a more circumspect view of the trajectory of historical consciousness, and assists us in understanding how science and religion have been interlaced from their very beginnings in creating and driving civilization's agenda. By so doing, we may yet "recover the memory of another, perhaps more compelling way to live," informing a new mode of praxis. But, to Kant's earlier point, is it perhaps too late for such reform, and is the opposition simply too great?

*****

A Manmade Volcano in the Gulf

June 2010

    Causality, not unlike the concept of liability, is a funny thing. It can be slippery at times. That is why our world is chocked full of detectives, scientists, and lawyers. It requires finding the reasons behind an event, and then identifying the culprit, agent or otherwise responsible party for the outcome. And, as a matter of fact (no pun intended) our scientific methodologies (the natural as well as the human sciences) beg us always to seek logical (i.e., causal) connections between events. But, what was the cause of the countless lives destroyed from the earthquake that rocked Port-au-Prince in Haiti? What triggered the volcanic eruption in Iceland disrupting so many travelers worldwide? What was responsible for the flood of oil unleashed deep within the Gulf of Mexico that has begun to decimate the ecosystem and destroy the livelihood of local populations? What triggered the global financial meltdown and the loss of so much equity? What unleashed the uprisings in Iran and Greece? How do we go about determining cause or assigning culpability?

I hear my critics already complaining that we must first make a distinction between natural disasters and man-made tragedies or failures. Such a complaint reminds me of the now-tired debate on global-warming. My critics continue unimpeded: the volcanic eruption in Iceland is simply a natural disaster happening without human influence... there is no culpability there. These same critics will go on to argue that scientists and engineers can cite various physical explanations for the explosion on the oil platform in the Gulf, thereby locating the cause for the disaster in a defective valve, a bad weld, methane in the tubing, or another series of events. And on that basis they can assign blame or liability for the gusher to a responsible party.

As good scientists – well equipped by our rationalistic upbringing – we always look for the appropriate causes to specific events. Natural disasters are, by definition, not manmade; manmade disasters imply human responsibility or culpability. But technology, and its handmaiden – modern science – have made it their mission to continuously enhance and increase our control over nature, to bend it to our will. So where does the natural stop, and the manmade – the cultivated, the artificial –begin? Is not what's left of "nature" itself now under the direct or indirect influence of human activity? Does not Lorenz's "butterfly effect" hold true between these two realms as well as within each, as Robert Redford reminded us in the 1990's movie *Havana*?

A butterfly can flutter its wings over a flower in China and cause a hurricane in the Caribbean...

Certainly human activity is at least as far reaching in its influence as that of a butterfly. Does not a banking failure in the USA effect the financial health of the global economy?   Does not our aggressive and violent interventions on the earth – beneath it, above it, and within it – have an impact upon climatological, geological and other natural events and occurrences?   Of course they do, just as surely as the institutions of our political economy and culture have a controlling influence upon individual behaviors, global economies and social relations.

Does nobody see the possibility that the "spill" in the Gulf, the global financial meltdown, recent mining disasters in the USA and Russia, earthquakes, budding insurrections, and other political unrest are linked? Even causally related? We have tried hard to control the earth as much as we have worked continuously to control one another. And perhaps BP was only the delivery boy in this instance, with the real message coming directly from Mother Earth herself, as one blogger has suggested: "You want oil? Here, I'll give you some fucking oil."   Is it wholly unreasonable to suppose that the earth reacts to our efforts to contain, control, and manipulate it, just as individual citizens react to similar efforts to subdue, domesticate and control them?

In truth, we are all to blame for the apocalyptic nightmare unwinding now in the Gulf. As hard as it may be to admit, it is our lifestyle – the expectations and demands we make upon nature and one another – that has caused this tragic calamity in the Gulf. We so desperately want (we even need) our cars, fishing boats, heated homes, air conditioning, new electronic toys – our comforts and distractions just to sustain ourselves in this increasingly artificial world we've collectively constructed. We ourselves have created and/or acquiesced to civilization and its self-proclaimed manifest destiny of domination… over nature and over one another. We need to take a serious look in the mirror and recognize our own culpability in these matters.

The alluvial soils of the Persian Gulf were apparently the nutritive beginnings of modern civilization; perhaps the Gulf of Mexico will herald its fast approaching, oil-choked ending. When we took those first careless steps out of the wilderness – away from the savannah, the desert, the forest, and the steppe – and began building cities to house the citizen-workers who would build our castles and other great institutions, those who would be fed with the produce from the newly cultivated fields and domesticated animals, this was the underlying, the initial cause of our spreading disasters and the madness we witness today.

Sure, volcanoes will happen, tsunamis occur; tornadoes, sinkholes, hurricanes, avalanches, earthquakes, and climate change are all events in the natural world. But who can say to what degree the manipulating, dominating, domesticating, and controlling machinations of human ingenuity do not effect, influence or trigger such "natural disasters?" We acknowledge, after all, that natural disasters often cause human suffering, including political, social, and economic turmoil. And certainly, the calamities (the death and destruction) caused by such events are directly related to the development of cities, permanent dwellings, and the many other fixed "institutions" of civilized life that stand to collapse under the weight of any such natural event. The devastation wrought is directly proportional to the concentration of populations enslaved to systems that monitor and control the human drama, the spectacle – the institutions that write and rewrite our histories, personal and collective.

We need *not* think long and hard about the connections, the cause of suffering brought on by disasters natural or human today. The sheer weight of civilization's assaults on the planet – technologically – are simply to much for the earth to bear, at least as much as its economic, political and social assaults on populations are too much for humanity to bear much longer. Mother Earth does get the last word in this debate, and it seems to me in these last several months that she has been speaking her mind, and getting a lot off of her chest. The question is: will the rest of us also make ourselves heard and take action before it is too late?

*****

On the Future of an Illusion: Pre 'Post Civilization' Blues

June 2010

It is fascinating to see what is happening now in the world. There seems quite a lot of disaffection with the way things are "progressing" - ecological crises all around, a global financial meltdown, peak oil, the growing drumbeat of war, insurrections popping up in all the worst places, unparalleled greed, apparently irrational terrorism, ethnic hostilities, and the evaporation of the American Dream like warm breath on a mirror. Even Mother Nature seems to be getting into the act with volcanoes, sinkholes, tornadoes, tsunamis, global warming. What's next? It's like the whole fricking thing is coming down around us all at once.

Barely two decades into America's uncontested ascendancy to the status of unipolar imperial power — with the entire planet apparently globalizing around our self-delusional spectacle of liberal democratic capitalism and its digital enclaves of techno-freakiness — and the whole thing starts to unwind. Planes are flying into skyscrapers, wars are popping up everywhere, terror is on the lips and in the minds of the populace, the world is eerily connected by virtual communities, the Euro zone is going under, Toyota is selling garbage cars, mini insurrections are flaring in Greece and the Persian Gulf, the Israelis have gone bonkers, North and South Korea are playing paddy cake again, and everybody is a news reporter, political analyst, or terrorist. Why, even some Joe nobody and Sarah know-nothing have become overnight national heroes.

Now, for those of you who think this makes the system vulnerable, well perhaps you're right. But don't believe for one moment you are going to take it down without a struggle. It will not come down by an act or even the collective acts of all the disgruntled middle class Americans and Europeans who have seen the light. There are centripetal forces holding it together as much as there are centrifugal forces pulling it apart. Aside from the controlling hands of the plutocracy, there is too much raw desire out there in the hinterlands of civilization, too many have-nots who have been living on the poverty stricken fringes of this beast just waiting their turn, and scratching for a piece of the elusive pie.

The entire Soviet Bloc, for example, was systematically and forcibly excluded from all the "fun" for almost a century. But the forbidden fruits are now within their grasp. And now the Chinese have finally woken up from their slumber as well and are quickly focused on putting a car in every one of their citizens' driveways. The Indians as well have decided they want to play in the game. In Mumbai they have made a good beginning by taking over all of the telephone customer service functions for most major American corporations. Not only that, but a majority of citizens in the West (the first world) have been living at or below the poverty line for generations. They too want a payday and a taste of the forbidden fruit.

The only way you're going to bring down Western civilization, its Curriculum and its Spectacle, is if you pry it from the dying hands of all these previously designated have-nots and the plutocrats who own and manage it. You can see it in the younger generation of Siberians here in Barnaul. They cannot live without their cell phones, their iPods, their recently financed cars and newly minted driver's licenses. They are tasting the promise of the spectacle, and they are mesmerized by its elusive appeal. It is not just blue jeans they want... they want it all!

So what about those of us who have this sense of *ennui* today, this feeling of pre post-collapse blues? How do we act on this feeling and prepare for the reality of a post-collapse world? First, if we think that we can somehow return to the Garden, how things were before the rise of civilization - back to the life of a hunter-gatherer - we are ourselves delusional. The conditions for the possibility of a return no longer exist. The land bases have been destroyed: raped and depleted of their natural flora and fauna. Moreover, the tools of civilization have become too much like a second skin for any of us to let go of them so easily, if at all. Rousseau was right when he said that civilization replaces our natural instincts with other, newer one's, without which we cannot long survive in civil society. So, to prepare for such a return would be a fool's errand.

However, it does seem that our current course is unsustainable, and will eventually consume itself in its own greed and shortsightedness. So, what does one do in this state of malaise, living with the pre post-collapse blues?

The most likely piece of advice is to find a small piece of manageable land in the more northern climes. This assures you that most freeloaders from the collapse won't bother you. They will most likely head south, where it is warmer, thinking life should be easier there. But when global warming really sets in the north will be a paradise (relatively speaking), the south more like hell. And you will be sitting in the catbird's seat, so to speak.

Next, it may be good to learn how to fish, hunt, and grow your own vegetables. Also, learn how to forage for mushrooms, berries, and nuts in the forests. A course in naturalism might be advisable. Make sure you understand which foods are edible and which are not when going into the forest.

Begin simplifying your life; wean yourself off of technology - computers, television, stereos and cell phones. Learn how to live without it all. Automobiles! Hah, that's a joke. There won't be any gas or oil around to run them. Remember Mad Max!! Bicycles may be a good source of transportation for short distances. But, then, you may be wiser learning how to enjoy life in the forest, the cave or your small cottage if you've prepared one that's easily maintainable.

Try to locate a good source of drinking water to set up your outpost. And whatever you decide to do, do it with someone you trust and care for, and who cares deeply for you. You will need that security, because that will be all you get. A small tribe or perhaps a clan of loosely related, like-minded folk would be a good idea. The prospective anarchy that will follow the collapse of civilization will not resemble in the least the primal anarchy of egalitarian tribes of hunter-gatherers that preceded the fall into civilization.

This post-collapse anarchy may more truly resemble Hobbes' war of all against all. It is best to be prepared; or perhaps, just let it be, and enjoy the moment!! After all, the moment is all we really have.

*****

I find it amusing that the Obama administration is seeking to prosecute alleged Russian "spooks" in the USA. But maybe it should not be a surprise. After all, we now understand that our regime is no less prone to the dramatic than the most tenacious of theocracies, and equally as paranoid.

A few months back I wrote how this administration had hired a Dr. Cass Sunstein to head the Department of Information and Regulatory Affairs. An academic, Dr. Sunstein had previously proposed creating a division of "thought police" to monitor the Internet, snoop and infiltrate the diverse blogs that might be undermining the "official" view of things, and covertly redirect discussion to how we should be interpreting affairs and policies at home and abroad. According to Sunstein, it is important to limit or reverse the impact of the heterodox or weird views freely-flowing through the virtual milieu such blogs create. So now Obama has decided to create a new piece of legislation allowing the Feds to "turn off" the Internet for up to four months at White House discretion (without Congressional oversight) under a new Emergency Powers Act by means of an Internet "kill switch" bill.

So in the midst of establishing a legal framework for these clandestine domestic activities and policies, and certainly in what might appear as an attempt to distract our attention from further erosion of those elusive freedoms we believed we had, the CIA has discovered Russian spies in our midst. Oh my God! What do you think they are looking for here? A quick fix to the financial crisis, our recipe for domestic economic disaster, a legal framework for shutting down the Internet in Russia, or perhaps the proper way to constitute their own secret thought-police?

Look folks, I have said this before. All governments are similarly constituted at bottom - they want to consolidate power, expand its influence globally, and shut down any dissent. They don't give a damn about anything else.

Let us see, weren't we wagging our morally superior finger at Iran's theocracy for attempting to shut down the Internet last summer during their contested elections? Then, did we not look judgmentally askance at China for censoring Google and its Internet activities in that authoritarian state? Are we no different than these command and control nations? The truth is we are no different. We just cloak things in a language of fairy tales and nationalism that let's us believe that we are different, superior, more free than those other folk. Truth. We are not.

We must begin to look clearly and without illusions at our nation, any nation - at the State and its true nature. The only difference between civilized nations is the stories they tell to their people to help them feel comfortable within the straight jacket of the political system that has been established to control them. Some stories are more successful; others not so much. Some states (nations) are more bureaucratic than others. Some are more forgiving in one area of social or commercial activity than another. But all regimes basically seek to keep us under their thumb by feeding us enough of a story that we remain anesthetized to the reality of what they are doing.

What do you all think is going on with the eruption of crude in the Gulf? Do you think we are privy to the truth? Of course not! They tell us only what we need to know - which isn't much. It is not just BP that is not forthcoming. Our government also withholds information to suit its needs at the moment.

Tell me folks, where did we get with healthcare for all Americans; and without the threat of jail or bail for not making our commercial insurance payments? Where did we get with financial reforms and making those greedy bastards pay for destroying the global financial system? Where are we in the Gulf? What gives? Why is the federal government trying to silence dissenting opinion in this country? Why will there be an agency to support the suppression of bloggers they don't like?

Actually, they cannot address any of these officially. It is not the business of government to enrich or enhance the populace or its overall intelligence, but only to craft good citizens and embolden its owners and leaders. It is in the nature of the State to suppress dissident opinion, to silence those who would question its legitimacy. Don't look for solutions here, my friends. Here there are only the cold hard facts of civilized politics.

*****

July 2010

Between the 27,000 abandoned oil wells in the Gulf of Mexico, an unwinable war in Afghanistan, and a host of other domestic and international policy issues staring us in the face, perhaps we now can see that there is really only one motivation behind even the most "forgiving" of political entities: extract wealth from wherever you can find it, and spread your influence far and wide. Superpower is simply a modern term for empire and hegemony.

America's unrestrained drive for hegemonic influence over the entire globe is now obvious, even to its citizens and economic slaves. (It has been obvious to the rest of the human community for quite some time.) And our leadership's desire to take control of any available natural resources in the process is a given; be it drilling holes in the floor of the Atlantic Ocean or "nation building" in Iraq and Afghanistan while destroying countless lives in the process. Everything is justified, as long as it is a good investment, politically or economically. [See Richard Haass, in Newsweek, "Rethinking Afghanistan: We're not winning. It's not worth it."]

What do we want from the Middle East? We want their rich mineral deposits, cheap labor, and new markets for our products and the dissemination of our cultural distractions. Our goals have become so obvious that our lack of shame and embarrassment only emboldens those who rail against us. Our State, the American Empire, is no more altruistic than those nations run by erstwhile banana-republic dictators. In fact, our self-proclaimed moral authority and our aggressiveness in such endeavors makes our behavior that much more reprehensible.

But, that is the nature of the State - of civilized political society. And in such a society, even if it be called a democracy, there is no voice for the people. The hierarchy - economic, social and political - silences all opposition, one way or another. The masses have no money and no voice. And those officials elected to represent the people are mere puppets of the ruling plutocratic-oligarchy.

Bottom-line, there is very little difference between a fascist, communist or democratic-capitalist regime in this respect. The means of control might differ, and perhaps in some important respects at times. But the objectives, and now more often than not even the means, are showing increasing similarities: homeland security, Administrative "thought police," Internet censorship, the exhaustive enumeration of laws by which to control us and punish us.

Yes, I know, what we say. We say that we are a nation of laws. By default, that means the law comes first... not the person. It is a life lived in the abstract, and in obedience to an infinite number of abstract legal requirements most of which have little to do with securing individual rights or recognizing individual worth; rather it is a life dedicated to protecting the sovereign, the corporation, and the ongoing life of the nation - all three, abstract entities.

What we want, as a nation, never was and is not now sustainable. It is an ill-gotten prize, won on the backs of all our citizens and all those we "conquer" as we seek to spread our influence - politically, economically, and culturally. And it is not only other human lives that we destroy, but the lives and living spaces of countless other species cohabiting this planet alongside of us.

*****

A Rectification of Names: Truth and Freedom of Speech

December 2010

"During times of universal deceit, telling the truth becomes a revolutionary act."   George Orwell

"We live in strange times." I hear this phrase often today. Given the nature of this apparent strangeness, it is perhaps necessary to clarify one's position – a kind of rectification of names, if you will. Simply put, I am a culture critic. I describe what I see in the social, political, and cultural milieu, and try to provide my readers with some perspective, an alternative to the commonly accepted view. I go behind the official version of the *Curriculum* to expose the framework informing it, although it is not always welcome.

I don't condone revolutionary activity. I fail to understand violence directed against the State; it's a pointless exercise that cannot possibly result in a positive outcome. It can only encourage and justify further countermeasures – acts of violence, belligerence, and repression — on the part of the State and its machinery. Honestly, was there any less hierarchical control of citizens after the revolutions in Russia, France or America than there was before? Such actions apparently only succeed in replacing one power hierarchy with another, perhaps more restrictive one.

Why feel compelled to take any action at all? Empires are already in the process of crumbling and civilization itself is collapsing of its own weight and inertia. Collectively, we have done so much irrevocable damage to the biosphere and its sensitive ecosystems, to flora and fauna alike, that our systems cannot function for much longer. We have rendered such irreparable damage to diverse species, including *Homo sapiens*, and most specifically to its indigenous populations, that such constant battering can only result, finally, in collapse.

So, there is no reason to fight against the hegemony; it can only provokes a response, and provide the State with more strength and greater legitimacy in the long run. As LaoTzu said, the best course of action is through non-action *(wei wu wei)* – to sit out the competition, let the disease run its course, and watch the spectacle unfold. Just be sure to find a safe place from which to enjoy the view. Because when things get rough, it could become dicey or dangerous. And while I am partial to the anarchist's point of view, I am cynical about his prospects. The anarchy that will likely emerge post-collapse will not be the peaceful, kinship-based egalitarian anarchy of pre-civilized clan and tribe; but more on the order of Hobbes' war of all against all.

But when the State — particularly an elected, purportedly democratic one — begins to treat any and every exercise in free speech or truth-seeking as a revolutionary act, as an act of espionage, it overplays its hand, undermining its own credibility, its own legitimacy, and betrays the underlying deceptions and deceptiveness of its core motives.

So, given my position, how would I judge the actions of Julian Assange and Wikileaks' role in the recent spate of finger-pointing we find animating divergent voices of this Administration and the body politic? Is he really a revolutionary, or, more boldly, a terrorist or anarchist, as some have suggested? After all, most of these labels flow from the mouths of those who are paid to know better. But are they not merely political deflections, all of them, calling names and creating straw men or red herrings wherever they can be useful in diverting attention from the truth? Truth. Now that's an interesting concept.

As I recall, our word for "truth" has a unique etymological history. It derives, rather circuitously, from the Greek *Lethe*, the river of forgetfulness, one of the five rivers of the underworld. The term *"lethe"* in classical Greek mythology literally means "oblivion", "forgetfulness," or "concealment." The Greek word for "truth" on the other hand, from whence we derive our own concept, is *aletheia*, meaning un-forgetfulness, unconcealment, or disclosedness. The event of truth would be taking something that was previously concealed or hidden and letting it shine-forth. What the Wikileaks people seem to be about is precisely this activity, *aletheia*... the disclosure or unconcealment of that which was previously hidden or concealed. They are, in brief, truth-seekers, in the sense we derive from its classical Greek origins.

The truth, as far as I can see it is as follows: Mr. Assange (while not technically a US citizen) is exercising a purported right among all apparently democratic regimes — the right to freedom of speech (unconcealment or disclosedness) as articulated in our own Bill of Rights. Second, he neither solicits nor pays for the information he receives. It is provided to his organization freely by whistleblowers that believe their employers are engaged in wrongdoing or otherwise committing ethical infractions that the whistler feels compelled to rectify. They too are truth-seekers, engaged in acts of unconcealment, of disclosedness *(aletheia)*. And, if I remember correctly, there was a time, not too long ago in this great country, when we were teaching our college graduates, particularly in the engineering curriculum where I worked, to understand their broader obligations to society, over and above obligations to some corporate owner or even government agency if it were engaged in wrong doing, and to report those abuses so as to get the conditions rectified.

But this begs a larger question: why is Julian Assange receiving so much material, and why now? The American people have never been big on rebellion or revolution (well except for that one-time thing with the British); and we have not even been very good on protesting (OK, maybe on Vietnam and briefly on civil rights). But there are historical and philosophical reasons for this. Slick marketing and even slicker politicians have convinced *We The People* that something called freedom exists in this country. And because we can drive our own cars from one state to another here with no constraints, because our passports are almost universally accepted around the world, the majority has believed that this freedom is something real. But this is not what constitutes freedom; the American people have been sold a bill of goods, not a Bill of Rights... and all the bills are finally coming due (pun intended).

So there is a growing sense among the body politic here that they have been paying for all of these charades and excesses long enough, and now they are going to exact payment from the real culprits. They are going after all the avarice, the greed, the pretension and self serving lies of the political class and corporate elites who run this country, and who have run it into the ground lording it over those have-nots who have nothing or very little left to lose. The middle class in particular, the workers of America, have awoken from *The Dream* and recognized that they have been living a nightmare, and they want it to stop. So they have taken matters into their own hands, and one by one they are sharing the dirty laundry of this country – its political, military and economic bullies – for the entire world to see.

Of course, those who are running the show, the elites and overlords whose unmentionables are being exposed, have a significant interest in withholding such information, so they will do whatever it takes to make it stop and silence the leakers. They tell us about "clear and present dangers;" they will talk about protecting State secrets, safeguarding our process, and ensuring the safety of American lives on the battlefield and abroad. So they call this information-release espionage, treason, even terrorism. And they are seeking to punish the whistleblowers severely; they will try to close down Assange's shop anyway they can, resorting to whatever methods are at hand, applying pressure, economically, politically and militarily upon its own constituencies, its colleagues, and its allies internationally; they will try to tuck Julian Assange away for good in some dark off-shore prison, if they only could.

As I said, it is in the nature of the State to fight any apparent rebellion or protest with increasing oppression, repression and aggression. Ironically, such increased repression will only exacerbate the State's own headlong rush off the cliff. Nietzsche was not wrong my friends when he wrote:

Only where the State ends, there begins the human being who is not superfluous; there begins the song of necessity, the unique and inimitable tune. Where the State ends - look there, my brothers!

******

Phenomenology and the Crisis of Civilization

January 2011

Because such fingers need to knit that subtle knot, which makes us man... (John
Donne, *The Ecstasy*)

I

With these dozen or so words the sixteenth century British metaphysical poet, preacher, and elegist, John Donne, foreshadowed the core challenge haunting our late post-modern world, while at roughly the same time a French philosopher and mathematician, Rene Descartes, was busy laying its oft-heralded foundations. Today we are heirs to the one and, like our forebear Descartes, skeptical of the other.

Our current, hyper-rational post-industrial culture is indebted to Cartesian doubt, along with its skeptical bifurcation of subject and object, mind and body, self and world. But this foundation itself rests upon prior constructions laid down by Aristotle and before him by the Greek Stoics. And even the categories of these ancients germinated in soils hearkening back yet further in human history, to the earliest divisions of labor and specializations that emerged with the burgeoning of urban life and the pre-reflective creation of institutional hierarchies six millennia ago. Its legacy is the syllogism, and the post-modern, hyper-rational State of today.

With the enforced separation of an objective, externalized universe, presumably independent of the knowing and contemplating subject, scientific hypothesis formation was able to provide us with a cache of new tools and an ever-expanding toolbox allowing us to manipulate and finally control that external environment. Such a set of tools would eventually be applied not only to objective nature, so conceived, and to those wild creatures populating the natural world, but to human beings as well. So our control and manipulation would finally extend to the very "soul of those who were by nature our own equals... our fellow men" *(Augustine, de Doctrina Christiana)*.

It was not until early in the twentieth century, with the work of Maurice Merleau-Ponty, another French philosopher, that the wrong turn initiated by Descartes was made clearly evident to trained philosophers. An earnest student of phenomenology and psychology, and with an uncanny commitment to the primacy of perception, Merleau-Ponty was able to disclose the fleshy "intertwining" of the sentient subject and the earthly sensuous, in short, the "body-subject (*le corps-sujet*), and the world-as-lived-by-the-body. It is this philosophical recollection of the inter-animation of body and world that may assist us in understanding the roots of our current crisis today – the global crisis of European (i.e., Western) Civilization.

II

We "first-worlders" tend to believe that our sciences and our technologies represent the best human ingenuity has to offer, that they demonstrate our unquestionable historical advancement and justify our global supremacy. We feel that we have overcome the more primitive and undeveloped aspects of the origins of our species, which, not in the least, is demonstrated through our increasing mastery over nature. In his *Introduction to Metaphysics*, Martin Heidegger challenges this very assumption of the modern temperament.

The fundamental error that underlies [modern sciences, natural and human] is the opinion that the inception...is primitive and backward, clumsy and weak. The opposite is true. The inception is what is most uncanny and mightiest. What follows is not a development but flattening down as mere widening out... a perversion of what is great, into greatness and extension purely in the sense of number and mass. The uncanniest is what it is because it harbors such an inception in which, from over-abundance, everything breaks out at once into what is overwhelming.... (165)

Here Heidegger overturns, as he frequently does, the commonly accepted view of things. This world of ours, the product of modern science, rather than representing a development is really a regression – a truncation, abbreviation, and reduction of the original richness and fullness of Being to mere numerical coefficients, mere extensions in space-time. The world has become emptied out by modern consciousness, reduced in simplest terms to a set of mathematical equations or legalistic syllogisms.

In all his later work, Heidegger was possessed with this state of affairs and with the curious relationship obtaining between thinking, being, and truth. He came to see that the original nature of human dwelling, of our being-in-the-world, was covered over by the not-so-artful constructs of modern consciousness, and that the truth of Being lay hidden in our collective forgetfulness. In fact, he came to rely increasingly upon the concept of truth as unconcealment or disclosedness, seeking to articulate the original intertwining of thinking and dwelling – a condition of openness that he termed *Gelassenheit*. He recovered the concept of truth from its ancient roots in Greek myth, deriving rather circuitously from the word *Lethe*, the river of forgetfulness, one of the five rivers of the underworld in Greek mythology. The term *"lethe"* in classical Greek literally meant "oblivion," "forgetfulness," or "concealment." The word for "truth" on the other hand, from whence Heidegger rescues our own concept, is *aletheia*, meaning un-forgetfulness, un-concealment, or disclosedness. The event of truth would be exposing that which had been essentially concealed or hidden and letting it again shine-forth.

It is this condition of forgetfulness that Heidegger wants so desperately to reverse in his final writings; he wants to let-shine-forth what was forgotten and covered-over at the origins of modern thought even prior to Aristotle. It is for this reason that he looks to Greek mythology and to the pre-Socratics to help excavate the ground of this forgetting, and begin to uncover the rich origins of human dwelling, and our primal openness (*Gelassenheit*) to the mystery of *Dasein* or Being-there.

III

But, it was with Maurice Merleau-Ponty's work that the locus of human dwelling was finally rediscovered philosophically, recovered from the oblivion of Western rationalism, scientism and metaphysics. It was his relentless focus on *le corps sujet* (the body-subject) that broke open that mysterious *chiasm*, the foundational "intertwining" of my body with the world-as-lived (*my flesh, the flesh of the world*), affording the very possibility of sentient experience — of touching and being touched, of seeing and being seen, of hearing and being heard, of smelling and being smelled, of tasting and being tasted (*The Visible and the Invisible*).

More important yet was his analysis of the problematic of unidirectional time, helping to break the spell of historical consciousness that had been cast like a pall over humanity for nearly six millennia. No longer were we to be chained to the treadmill of clock time's forward march. As he wrote in *The Phenomenology of Perception*:

We say that time passes or flows by. We speak of the course of time. The water that I see rolling by was made ready a few days ago in the mountains, with the melting glacier... If time is similar to a river, it flows from the past towards the present and the future. The present is the consequence of the past, and the future of the present. But this often repeated metaphor is in reality extremely confused. For, looking at the things themselves, the melting snows and what results from this are not successive events, or rather the very notion of event has no place in the objective world... if I consider the world itself, there is simply one indivisible and changeless being in it... The objective world is too much a plenum for there to be time. (411-412)

"...Too much a plenum for there to be time?" More than a challenging metaphor, this statement appears to be an indictment of Enlightenment hypothesizing and post-Enlightenment reasoning. Perhaps a not so indirect allusion to Descartes and Newton (*De Gravitatione*), Merleau-Ponty's words here suggest a fundamental overturning of our now common sense view, while recollecting the pre-reflective nature of human dwelling within the fullness (*plenum*) of the lived-body-world, what he later calls "the *thickness of the pre-objective present*, in which we find our bodily being, our social being, and the pre-existence of the world." (421, italics mine)

Merleau-Ponty seemed aware that there is something hidden or forgotten underlying our mundane experience of this reconstituted and modified environment; something linking us to the earth we inhabit and enlivening our presence here — something more primal than the hypotheticals of space and time generated by our scientists and our specialists.

IV

Heidegger as well understood that the emergence of scientific hypotheses concerning pure extension and temporal duration, and so our common sense conceptions of space and time, represented abstractions, transformations and perversions of a more primal and overwhelming experience of Being — perhaps what the Pacific Islanders referred to as "mana." For the Islanders, there was apparently no such thing as empty space or simple, objective material extension, as was the documented case among many other pre-urban tribes and hunter-gatherer societies; their world was filled with living, animate, sentient and powerful subjectivities lurking everywhere and residing almost anywhere – in the wind, the water, the stone, or the bush. (We first-worlders called it, condescendingly, animism.) So too, there is good reason to suggest that indigenous tribes had no genuine concept of pure linear duration either, no *time*, as we have come to know it, flowing from past to future (e.g., Dorothy D. Lee, *Freedom and Culture*). The natural cyclicality of life breathed around, through, and within them: the rising and setting of the sun, the lunar cycle, seasonal changes, the repetition of ritual archetypal behavior. In Heidegger's terms what happened with the emergence of thought from these auspicious and pregnant beginnings was a "flattening out" of an originally uncanny and overwhelming primal moment.

To this day there are some excellent studies that correctly point to the spread of agriculture and the birth of cities as the principal focus of our changed *material* relations with the world. Yet even these analyses typically make the underlying and pre-thematic assumption that the perceptions and consciousness of our preliterate, pre-civilized predecessors were roughly identical to our own; that we perceive the same world and experience our place therein as did our "primitive" forebears. But to infer that primal humans reasoned and conceptualized as we do today would be an unsustainable inference (see Owen Barfield, *Saving the Appearances*). Indeed, the opposite assumption is more likely the case; that they reflected quite differently on the *plenum* and on themselves than we do, and that this was in large measure a result of how differently they perceived and felt themselves within the world. There is certainly nothing in the anthropological, paleontological, or ethnographic record that would contradict such an assumption. In fact, there may be much, both in mythology and ethnography, to recommend it (for example, Mircea Eliade, *Cosmos and History*, Daniel Everett, *Don't Sleep, There Are Snakes*).

Specifically, our conceptions of pure extension and duration, of mere materiality and unidirectional time, themselves conceptually linked to a reification and radicalization of an objective and internalized sense of self –

removed from the world and observing it from afar – locked us into a specific place in history and to our own unique histories; this is a large part of that *difference*, and this is largely responsible not only for the emergence of civilization, but for the evolving crisis we now face. It is to this primeval transformation of consciousness that we must look for the inchoate but emergent beginnings of our crisis, even at the misty origins of Western Civilization.

V

There appears now to be a fork in the road we are traveling; but since, as we have suggested, the present is all we really have, there is not much sense in talking about having passed the point of no return. So, while the culture itself may appear to be locked in a self-inflicted death spiral, each of us still has a choice. Let's briefly consider the options.

On the one hand, we could simply do nothing at all and allow calendrical time, the relentless march of civilized history, to define us and continue its course unabated. In other words, we can maintain our commitment to this ancient trajectory that was set in motion as far back as Sumer, codified later by Aristotle, and more fully articulated in the Enlightenment and beyond; or we can personally choose to minimize or even terminate our participation in the unfolding spectacle, and find a more compelling way of being-in-the-world.

This brings us to the second option – recollection. We can each personally make an effort to recollect that genetic memory trace, recalling from within the hiddenness and forgetfulness of our own isolated egos the "subtle knot" that grounds our primal intertwining with the world-as-lived-by-the-body. In this way we might experience again that feral (wild) openness which first made the earthly sensuous and our own sentience possible.

The bigger challenge is for the collective, and the footprint we have made as a civilization. There have been global reverberations from this change of perception and consciousness that were set in motion so many millennia ago. There has been ecological, social, psychological, and economic fallout. How do we find a footpath back from those hypotheses, both social and natural scientific, that have led us to this point and continue to bind us collectively to this spectacle? It seems to me that Merleau-Ponty's reflections, while necessary for understanding the specific gravity of our *situated* presence, may not be sufficient for overcoming our current dilemma and slowing down or reversing its momentum or its negative effects. But perhaps with some effort we can yet find something that will at least reduce this cold tyranny of reason and its brainchildren – the syllogism and the modern State.

> *State is the name of the coldest of all cold monsters... State, where the slow suicide of all – is called 'life.'* [Nietzsche, *Thus Spoke Zarathustra, The New Idol*]

******

The Language of Crisis and The Crisis of Language

February 2011

In the wake of social and political upheavals now spreading like wildfire throughout Northern Africa and the Middle East, we hear noble slogans and soothing words about the will of the people being expressed and their desire for democratization. We find such sentiments slipping comfortably from the lips of Western politicians and splattered across the pages of our presses, as they seek to reassure us that this is just the natural longing of the human spirit to participate in our ideals of democracy and free markets. There is a concerted effort on the part of our elites to paint these events as an endorsement of Western values and lifestyle. But what exactly do these calming references to 'freedom' and 'democracy' denote coming from our elite? And are the changes these diverse populations seek really consistent with the worldview and values of the West? In light of these questions, it is appropriate to consider the role of language today, and particularly the challenge it poses with respect to the discomfort underlying current global upheavals.

In the slogans alluded to above, as is the case with much communication today, one might notice how there is quite a bit of talk but very little being said? Well, it's true. Language has been truncated, if not trivialized in the modern world, stripped bare of its depth and power. Where words once were heard as pregnant with signification, in our rationalized, digitized, and abridged vocabulary of the West all that has changed for the worst. Now a strictly calculating and logistical principle holds sway. Words have been reduced to mere symbols in an equation, placeholders in a syllogism, each having a single unambiguously identifiable referent, and only one. A must equal A, and it can never equal B; let alone A, B and C all together at once. There must only be one precise "signified" for each "signifier" - everything disambiguated - following both the formal demands of objective science and the legalistic requirements of hierarchical control.

But if you look back into the obscure and shadowy origins of language, you will find that before the written word there was only speaking, with oral traditions passed down from generation to generation. The written word emerging a little less than six thousand years ago, only fully appeared coincident with the birth of cities, with the organization of empires and their apparatus -- with civilization and history. We began making history only when we began to write that history!

This was another momentous invention of domesticated life. With the birth of cities on the heels of big agriculture, it was necessary to develop uniform (if not abstract) systems of economic, social, and political control to handle the gathering together of diverse and unrelated village, clan and tribal members, now as urban strangers - within and well beyond the city walls. This demanded a severe change in the nature of human communication, including the removal of polysemic ambiguity inherent in primal speech, and the articulation of a strictly univocal, disambiguated, written code.

Such linguistic rationalization was only effected with the invention of the syllogism, early on perfected by the Greeks, and recast by scientists, legislators, and politicians down through the ages. According to syllogistic reasoning, universal statements were to be related to particular circumstances within a coherent structure leading to unambiguous legal and scientific conclusions. So it all came down to "precise words and correct syntax...that is where social laws [were] made and natural laws [were] made or discovered" (Bram, *The Recovery of the West*).

But long before such sweeping linguistic changes took hold, our pre-historical speaking and proto-historical writing were much involved with myth. Passed on from originally oral sources, myth had a textural depth, ambiguity, and resonance that was still packed with meaning. Not only did the mythic word call up multiple referents, but also the copula between those diverse referents was extremely strong. To speak the name of something was in fact to invoke its existence, to experience its power as fully present. It was not then as it is now, where a metaphor or a simile merely suggests something else. For a preliterate gatherer-hunter, to identify your totem was to become one with it, and to feel the presence of your clan animal within you.

Even revisiting one of the earliest known written languages, Old Kingdom Egyptian, one finds oneself immersed within a polysemous, poly-textural world whose non-alphabetic characters still bear this sort of weight and significance. Hieroglyphic writing retained almost as much multi-referential power as did the preliterate word of far-older, oral traditions. Hieroglyphs not only allowed of multiple meanings; they also embodied the power of the signifieds within the signifier, whether it was etched on a tablet, a sarcophagus, or the temple wall.

Such was the wealth, potency, and openness of primal tongues. Over millennia of civilization, these languages were destroyed, forced into univocity and impotence. Stripped of their resonant depth, words were flattened-out under the cold and calculating logic of imperial and imperious histories. Words became slaves to the exacting requirements of syllogistic reasoning, eventually defining the direction of all civic life – social control grounded in rigid laws and specious principles artfully constructed to protect increasingly arrayed power hierarchies.

Chris Hedges has correctly noted that empires often communicate in two languages, one of imperatives and decrees, the other employing a gentler vocabulary of transcendent values and high-sounding ideals. Yet, they both do violence and are controlling in their own right, leading ultimately to the same end - disempowering the body politic ("Recognizing the Language of Tyranny," *Berserk Magazine*). So just maybe in their hearts and in their ears, the peoples to our east have finally identified one source of their suffering -- in the words they hear and the relentless assault of syllogisms that keep them enslaved within a language of violence.

Of course, I am not suggesting that the Egyptian people (or others) have rebelled against their regimes due to the loss of rich oral traditions. Their burning issues likely have much more to do with their bellies than with their tongues. But perhaps the political and economic deprivations imposed by such hierarchies have been masked by a linguistic straightjacket foisted upon citizens increasingly forced to live in a world made empty by the word as much as by threat of the sword.

A key catalyst of today's "global crisis" may be found in this emptying out of language, leading inexorably to an emptying of human experience - a hollowness that finds its only fulfillment in the proliferation of novel distractions and diversions as they consume and ravage all available resources, leaving nothing of value in their wake. Or perhaps, it finds solace only in rebellion. It is worth considering especially in light of Hedges final warning about any "centralized power."

American democracy [itself]… looks real even as the levers of power are in the hands of corporations... It too communicates in two distinct languages, that is until it does not have to, at which point it will be too late.

*****

Full Metal Jacket: Protecting The Homeland

May 2011

While our politicians seem hell-bent on making us feel safe from the bad guys, most Americans sense that this "war on terror" has put some real kinks in our experience of freedom here in the "homeland." But what it may have done is inadvertently expose the pretense of freedom under which we have been laboring for these many years, perhaps centuries. Perhaps it has succeeded in outing the underlying motive beneath our politics, its maneuverings and behind-the-scenes deal making, whether with big business, lobbyists or private contractors. Maybe it has betrayed the prime motivation beneath all political systems - power, its control, and aggrandizement.

Well, I imagine we will soon begin to see things more clearly. The full force and impact of the Obama presidency is on its way to the light of day, straight through the corridors of darkness and the possible instantiation of a domestic "thought police."

Of course, we can thank W and his troupe for starting us down this path, with passage of legislation allowing more flexible wire tapping rules and other "homeland security" measures intended to infringe upon our so-called civil liberties. But Obama is doing more than his fair share in escalating the endeavor.

After having given his nod to fines and jail time for citizen non-compliance with health-care reform legislation, Obama has tipped his hand to the next challenge, making sure all of us citizens believe what we are told by his administration, and do as we are asked by those in power.

I believe it was George Orwell who first raised the specter of the "thought police" in his novel, 1984. In Orwell's horrifying proleptic vision, it was the job of this agency to uncover and punish thought-crimes using a host of covert psychological and surveillance techniques to find and eliminate members of society whose very thoughts were challenging to the controlling hegemony.

Well, Obama is about to make Orwell's vision a reality for the homeland in 2010. His pick to head the Office of Information and Regulatory Affairs (OIRA), Dr. Cass Sunstein, Harvard Law Professor, proposed such an agency in a 2008 article published in The Journal of Political Philosophy.

Professor Sunstein, affectionately called (but not to his face) "Mr. Sunshine," wrote in "Conspiracy Theories: Causes and Cures," that such theories pose "real risks to the government's antiterrorism policies," stemming as they do from a "crippled epistemology." What he means by this is that conspiracy theorists have limited or poor information. His cure is to infiltrate these ill-advised groups with independent undercover agents (reporting to and paid by the administration) to correct the knowledge base of their disparate, renegade followers. As the article states:

Government agents (and their allies) might enter chat rooms, online social networks, or even real-space groups and attempt to undermine percolating conspiracy theories by raising doubts about their factual premises, causal logic or implications for political action. [20]

In this manner, he hopes to undermine the credibility and internal coherence of these heterodox groups. It is worth noting that Sunny, a Harvard Law Professor, has already been criticized publicly as a potentate for implementing censorship, online and elsewhere. It is Soviet style propaganda, plain and simple folks. And Mr. Sunshine has been in the news as recently as April and May of this year. As the April article suggests:

Reading between the lines of Sunstein's research paper, I believe it's "justified" to ask whether the Obama administration took Sunstein's "main policy idea" and put it into practice. If so, then We the People may likely pay for bureaucrats to engage in "counterspeech and marshal arguments" against us. We may pay, directly or indirectly, for "credible private parties to engage in counterspeech" (FactCheck, Media Matters, Snopes, public relations firms, progressive operatives who appear on CNN, FOX, CNBC, MSNBC and call into talk radio show, minions who write op-eds and letters to the editor, or "obots" who comment on blogs). Or we may merely pay for informal communication with such parties, encouraging them to "help." Did we pay for the secret meetings wherein someone organized media groups like Journo-list? We certainly paid for those organizing phone conferences between administration staffers and the NEA, which aimed to recruit artists to "help" promote the Obama agenda.

And this brings us full-circle to last week's post, reminding us again about the commodification of social policy, and the marketing of the State's overarching agenda to the populace. Stand aside China, America is in lock step, or is that goose-step, with your sentiments about Google and censorship. Whether it is direct or "inverted" (Chris Hedges), the creeping and covert totalitarianism of our state belies the fascist tendencies of all states. Nietzsche was correct; there is no truth and no freedom where there is political society.

State is the coldest of all cold monsters. Coldly it tells lies...in all tongues of good and evil... State, where the slow suicide of all is called 'life.' [Kaufmann, 160-1]

Politicians have one concern (no matter what they tell the public); and that is protection and expansion of power. Obama is no different than W. And the USA is no different than Russia, Venezuela, Cuba, China, Iran or North Korea.

We are moving slowly, but definitively into a police state. If you refuse to buy health insurance or if you even think the wrong thoughts, you are an enemy of the state. My friends, by writing this article, I am already labeled a heretic. I am already singled out as a potential problem to be solved or silenced.

Sunstein is now proposing a method of officially dealing with what he calls "dangerous" ideas, by claiming that the government could, "ban conspiracy theorizing," or "impose some kind of tax, financial or otherwise, on those who disseminate such theories". In short, Sunstein wants strong, official censorship, backed by threats of legal punishment, for those whose ideas he views as "dangerous" ...

The siren song is getting louder as we approach the Scylla and Charybdis of our own historic destiny; do not be fooled by its enticements. We are doomed as long as there is someone telling us what to believe and how to live our lives: someone who knows nothing of us personally - our suffering, our longing, our simple pleasures and our needs. This is especially so when all the maneuvering is behind the scenes, part of the scaffolding holding up the Spectacle. We are all heterodox thinkers my friends; one and all, conspiracy theorists (or worse: terrorists) in Sunny's view. The time to reflect is over. The time to make your voices heard is at hand. Or should we just retreat to the toilet and put a gun in our mouth?

Only where the state ends, there begins the human being who is not superfluous; there begins the song of necessity, the unique and inimitable tune. Where the state ends - look there, my brothers! [Kaufmann, 163]

*****

Resistance As Commodity: America Medicated and Enslaved

April 2011

We have all sat enthralled by the recent images dancing across our HD TVs, our PC and Notebook screens, as events have unfolded in the Middle East and Northern Africa over the past few months. From Morocco, Algeria, Tunisia and Egypt to Bahrain, Yemen, Syria, Saudi Arabia and Jordan, a surge of popular uprisings has appeared before us in brilliant and revolutionary Technicolor - the actions themselves having become spectacular commodities for our collective consumption. Better than reality television, we sit engrossed in these unfolding media spectacles.

But that is not all. We have also been quick to adopt as our own the frequent refrains we are fed by our media pundits and political leaders concerning the interpretation of such events. Their drumbeat is incessant: these enslaved masses want freedom! They want choice! They want democracy! They want what we have in America! And we the people dutifully allow such assumptions to go unchecked while their irony escapes us. The facts are that America has long supported those very regimes against which the rebels are now fighting. The uprisings across MENA have become just another gimmick, another prop, another marketing tool for our own elite and their paid propagandists in a bid to suppress domestic unrest and opposition here in the homeland.

But this is not the end of the story. The US and its ad hoc coalition of co-conspirators have now gone further with this charade, claiming the moral high ground and inserting their own military muscle into that civil war in Libya. They have attacked a sovereign nation while the media mythology of a humanitarian mission continues unabated, faithfully echoing the talking points from our beguiling leader: that we are fighting for the liberation of our Muslim brothers and sisters who are longing to join the ranks of the free and reap the benefits of unbridled democratic capitalism. (BTW: It's a song whose basic theme sounds an awful lot like the Soviet regime not too many years ago claiming to be fighting for the liberation of its brothers in Afghanistan.) And we the people sit guilelessly in the back bleachers listening to the choir and accepting such pabulum as gospel from the church hymnal.

We still remain comfortably entombed, again perched in front of those omnipresent big screens, gawking at the protests in the Wisconsin State House, and other sympathetic rallies that emerged across the U.S.A. We watched the quaint antiwar demonstration in Washington D.C. last December (attended by none other than author, blogger and war correspondent Chris Hedges along with the infamous Daniel Ellsberg). And we are witness to the demonstrations planned for New York's Union Square, inveighing against the abuses of kleptocrats at Bank of America and other high-rolling, high-riding banksters. But, has the movement of resistance, the very act of defiance, of rebellion, itself not been co-opted in advance by the system that it is aimed at reigning-in or overturning?

As the Soviet émigré Mikhail Epstein pointed out many years ago in *Transculture and Society*: a society like ours, a culture that commodifies everything it touches, "is able to absorb and assimilate even revolutionary challenges [through] the mechanism of commodification." In this way, any radical challenge to the system is instantly transformed, "denial itself, turned into another commodity." Or, as Allan Bloom suggested with a slightly different twist in The Closing Of The American Mind, a liberal democracy is capable of taking even the most countercultural activities and absorbing them into the mainstream, transforming such acts into acceptable cultural practice – with appropriate rules, policies and procedures.

It is not an unreasonable bet that this is what happens time and again to the resistance movement in the United States. It is turned into a commodity to be hawked through new media like Facebook and Twitter, proffered for consumption by the mainstream corporate press, and corralled by the establishment of new political movements like the Tea Party gang. Resistance becomes hoodwinked and then mainstreamed; brought in under the Big Tent. Here we have the taming and suppression of the human spirit. Even in full battle mode, those seeking actual change have simply become a spectacle to be observed, tolerated, enjoyed, even lauded; then clicked off once the next commercial bursts onto our screens. So much for radical politics and real rebellion in America: even our most sacred acts of defiance, of insurgency, are now routinely transformed into *objets de arte, objets de cultura* – commodities to be used for entertainment, distraction and propaganda.

The entire apparatus of our culture – a "culture of make-believe" as Derrick Jensen has dubbed it – may be brought to bear at any moment in defusing resistance, not through authoritarian suppression or banana-republic brutality, but through more subtle means of control, persuasion and marketing: allowing it, praising it, and repackaging it for distribution to the public. This in turn further stabilizes and emboldens the system, reinforcing its faux image of cultural, political or religious openness. As Allan Bloom well noted, openness becomes the enemy of the good; but it also becomes the enemy of any real challenge to the system itself. Openness betrays its true nature, as a core element of that "inverted totalitarianism" that Chris Hedges is so fond of discussing these days.

Ours is a system that gives much lip service to openness, reform, and fairness; but in reality it is one in which real change has become a genuine impossibility. Unfortunately - and what Hedges may have missed in his own acts of resistance - even our best attempts at "disrupting" the State or its mechanisms are easily hijacked by the regime and quickly turned into political treasure. In other words, while the State's police forces and other Homeland Security thugs gingerly manhandle the rebels themselves (according to more or less agreed upon rules of engagement), the acts of rebellion are commoditized and re-packaged by the media, our politicians, and their puppet masters for general consumption by, and medication of, the populace.

In this way, any legitimate internal threats to the State are effectively disarmed through commodification and effective marketing. And the snake oil works! We demonstrate, we disrupt, we challenge, we take our lumps and go to jail for a night; and we think we are free and have a bona fide voice in how this entire show is produced. But the truth is they have us right where they want us; and us, what do we have? We have nothing but our medications and our enslavement to the State!

But, if you have any doubts about America's totalitarian allegiances or the commodification of our resistance to it, just look at the arrests in Washington D.C. last Sunday (April 10th) of those demonstrating against our militarization of Latin America and our material support for totalitarian dictators in MENA and elsewhere around the globe. In that bit of news we were spectators to an "annual event" of self-described "street theatre and artistic expression," including puppets and performances, as integral parts of the planned "die-in." If the American resistance movement has not been transformed into just another commodity - another distracting entertainment - of our society of the Spectacle, then I do not know what it has become. I did not see street theatre in demonstrations across Iran, Egypt, Tunisia, or Libya. And I do not now see artistic expressions on the streets of Bahrain. We should stop drinking the cool-aid my friends!

*****

In The Territory Of The Pleistocene: An Etiology Of Collapse

May 2011

When faced with a crisis it is always tempting to look back at our brief history and try to locate exactly where we went wrong and when things turned so sour. After all, this is what specialists of the discipline teach us: to seek out proximate causes for our current predicament in events of the recent past. And certainly we may learn a good deal from such analyses. But to understand our unfolding collapse - the global proportions of which we now all bear witness to - as a failure of politics in America, and specifically democratic liberalism, is shortsighted and myopic. Hoping to grasp the cause of this crisis, Chris Hedges asks in The Corporate State Wins Again, "When did the press, labor, universities and the Democratic Party... wither and atrophy?" As if their collective failures could have been the precipitating cause of our current global calamity.

The challenges we face today – global systemic failure, including ecological, economic, financial, social and political systems – are the later symptoms of a disease that took hold of the human community many millennia ago, long before the emergence of the modern State. The Corporate State or Corporate Capitalism, which Mr. Hedges points to as the loci of our recent descent, themselves have roots in the murky hinterlands of human history. Even Hedges alludes to this remote origin when he writes: "Human history, rather than a chronicle of freedom and democracy, is characterized by ruthless domination."

This ruthless and largely pathological lust to dominate - underpinning the Corporate State - was first given life with the establishment of institutional hierarchy and associated tools of command and control, casuistic law. Its footings were laid at the very dawn of historical consciousness, even before the Code of Hammurabi in Babylon. The earliest example may be the Code of Ur-Nammu written in Sumerian approximately 2100 BC, lying as a foundation stone of modern legal authority and the exercise of political power.

Such hierarchical authority, whose etiology can be traced to the first urban centers, creates its own unique form of sociopathy, attracting those 'infected' into its ascendant ranks and affording them a lofty plateau from which to survey and manipulate the subjugated masses. It provides those elevated elites with an illusion of separation, heightening their sense of self-worth and personal superiority. It is this self-induced fantasy that enables them to create laws, pass judgments, and execute decisions that apply to all but themselves. Just look at the actions of those in our Congress and in our courts, not to mention the sociopath-in-chief and his chorus-line of cohorts sitting just down the road from that august body of jurists and lobbyists. As Hedges aptly summarizes:

These elites do not have a vision. They know only one word—more. They will continue to exploit the nation, the global economy and the ecosystem. And they will use their money to hide in gated compounds when it all implodes. Do not expect them to take care of us when it starts to unravel.

In short, the entire charade of civil society, of institutional hierarchy – be it political, religious, corporate, or armed military (for god's sake) – the very scaffolding of the modern civilized State; all of these institutions are erected upon a singular foundation uniquely focused on enhancing command and control. That is the necessary outcome of a mode of reasoning and a logistic ushered in with the first cities approximately 6,000 years ago. It was then that the first statists drew together tens of thousands of 'citizens' (Ur had an estimated population of 65,000) – strangers, newly quartered within tightly packed city walls and satellite villages – all scratching to find a safe place on the growing animal farm. Civilization itself is the pathology; hierarchy, the pathogen.

But writers like Hedges, as astute a thinker as he is, fail to see this; or at least they do not care to admit it – that the problems we face have roots older than the past several hundred years. Hedges himself seems to believe that we can rehabilitate the system: that its institutions are salvageable and can be used for good and noble purpose. This is no doubt why he has chosen to engage in political theatre, in public demonstrations, in choreographed attempts at disrupting the machines of commerce and government. He still feels there is some way to keep this whole charade going, but now with healthier motives and public transparency. As if this would redirect or reverse the trajectory of our global collapse.

As Paul Shepard has pointed out, we are all creatures of the Pleistocene - a geological epoch spanning nearly two million years of proto-human and human prehistory. That is the environment in which the evolution and refinement of our own species, Homo sapiens, took place. The end of that epoch coincided by-and-large with the beginning of settled agriculture and the start of the Neolithic era at the opening of the Holocene epoch approximately 10,000 years ago. It was shortly thereafter that we witness the emergence of new forms of social organization, methods of food acquisition, the building of cities, and the rapid deployment of hierarchy throughout these emergent institutions. It was there that we lost our way on a footpath leading inevitably to the cult of the individual, along with its attendant rights and privileges - privatization, securitization, legislation, and the evolution of the modern State.

Part of the problem, I suspect, goes back to a similar reorganization of our sensorium that occurred concurrently with this new form of social organization, and the transition from a predominantly nomadic existence to more domesticated arrangements. There dawned a re-ordering of our senses, with sight grabbing top billing in another emerging hierarchy. Modern sedentary urban life now presents itself primarily as a visual field (like a screen) spread out in front of us for inspection. A Pleistocene world, on the other hand, was more aural and palpable; it surrounded one in sound and in the "earthly sensuous" – providing a rounder experience of the world-as-lived than that proffered by the visual maps we so cherish today. And, as the father of general semantics, Alford Korzybski, pointed out: "the map is not the territory." Territory is all encompassing; the map (again like the screen) is a simple visual representation.   Moreover, the visual event is predominantly linear in organization; with relatively marginal peripheral vision, we typically see only what is directly within our line of sight. The aural and tactile surround is more cyclical, encircling us; we can hear and even feel the predator that is stealthily approaching us from behind.   We begin to recognize now just how deprived and empty life in this modern jungle has become; an emptiness due largely to the eclipsing of the sensorium by the demands of civilized existence under the watchful eye of linear (historical) Father Time.

And this gets us to the heart of the matter. Perhaps we can emerge on the other side of collapse into a new world along the lines one fellow blogger recently suggested -- "decentralized societies organized around democratic communities and watersheds, with no standing armies, no more nation-states, no capitalism or macro-economies aside from loosely organized trade federations since some trade will be required." So much for the logistics; but can we overcome our unflinching epistemological commitment to vision, to the specter of unilinear time, and its existential implications - history, planning, progress, technological advancement, production, consumption, growth and domination?

Can we step back far enough to reclaim a more natural place within the animal kingdom? Can we recover from our early civilized need to dominate nature, and the substantial hangover that really came into its own with Francis Bacon, the scientific method, and our transition into the modern era of infinite progress?

This pathology, this disease, if you will, is a feeling of dis-ease with our own feral core, a cloak foisted upon us through 6,000 years of indoctrination to the new curriculum. But, modern Homo sapiens appeared almost 200,000 years ago, and the earliest species of our genus, Homo habilis, two million years back; all indications are that they lived less obtrusively in nature and with one another. And they lived without the terror of historical consciousness until its eruption with the birth of civilization. What the scholars will not tell us is that there was something substantial lost with the emergence of this new consciousness and the subsequent development of historical thought. Recovering this buried genetic memory trace must begin with a recapitulation to the subjectivity of our bodies and a reawakening of our sentient selves.

It is not a matter of moral turpitude that drives us mad... it is this madness (civilization) that drives us to apparent moral turpitude. Changing the perspective and agenda of modern society (and its sociopathic masters of the universe) is not an ethical or a religious matter; it is an epistemological, even an ontological matter - it cannot be achieved by imploring, cajoling, threatening or harming. It may not be do-able at all on a grand scale. It may just require that those who have rediscovered that inner feral core do what they can to prepare themselves for a post-collapse world, and try to enjoy the Spectacle unfolding around us.

*****

May 2011

Like a ghostly soldier of fortune, the shadow of our hegemony has been casting its pall over the earth for more than two centuries now; but it is growing thin, its pulse weakening, its days numbered. The American empire – this great experiment in freedom and prosperity – is apparently approaching its end; but the would-be corpse is still breathing, battling like a mythic hero desperate to stay alive.

Early indications of this eventuality were foreshadowed in global projections of peak oil along with the empire's continued environmental abuse and degradation. More recently, the hard-fall of its financial markets and idling of its economic engines betrayed undeniable signs that collapse was on course: the road of infinite progress and universal affluence picking up speed in a stunning reversal, now the road to perdition.

Barack Obama's selection signaled the rising of the curtain on possibly the final act, as another charismatic emperor struts onstage promising a new dawn with more growth, orchestrated around an ever-expanding imperial vision, with America again "ready to lead the world." (I'm sure I was not the only one who choked when those words left his lips). Even the least perceptive among the rag-tag proletariat out in the hinterlands could read the tea-leaves; America's weariness exposed, a looming archetypal battle brewing among forces of hegemonic expansion, contraction, and those instigating for something whispered only softly in kitchens and back alleys, its disintegration. Many began already back then to look for a safe exit.

Additional signs of collapse were the palpable, almost visceral reaction of individual States, recoiling from the growing burden of a constantly expanding Federal mandate. Perhaps the governors finally had enough, recognizing the insidiousness of this creeping imperial disease - relentlessly clawing its way forward - as clearly as others around the globe have seen our national character for more than a century. No less than two-dozen States have challenged health care overhaul and just this week urged a U.S. Appeals Court to strike down the legislation, arguing that it far exceeds the federal government's constitutional powers.

Additional evidence of national disintegration has been unmistakable over the past two years: a renewed defense of the 10th amendment – States seeking to safeguard their rights, vociferously refusing federal stimulus funds, with some backdoor chatter of secession in various quarters. And all this was coupled with an almost magically self-induced splintering strife haunting both factions (Democrat and Republican) of the controlling political hegemony.

It appears that much of this early maneuvering by the States arose in direct response to the Obama administration's move to curtail the second amendment's right to bear arms, nationalize certain commercial enterprises, make 'hand-cuff' loans to the States, and continue to support its multinational corporate sponsors' investments through expanded military campaigns globally. Well, you get the picture! More big government! More imperial control! More power!

President Obama tipped his hand early in his tenure during a visit to the Kremlin (of all places) not long after ascending to the high seat. Speaking to graduates of the New Economic School in Moscow in 2009, he stated, "The pursuit of power is no longer a zero-sum game... Progress must be shared." To clarify, the issue raised by such a bold admission is not whether this "pursuit" is a zero or positive sum game; but simply, that power is the name of the game plain and simple – a game played by hegemons for ensuring their global influence and driving their imperialist designs. The real import of his remark was not merely acknowledging that continual expansion is a cornerstone of nation building, but that the real game is the pursuit of power globally (we can worry later about win, lose or draw).

And, as we have seen, our imperialist elites will stop at nothing to gain the upper hand. They will sleep with, take orders from, or eliminate anybody in order to expand their reach and enrich themselves, no matter what the cost to the earth, our citizenry, or other cultures: conspiring with the likes of BP, Goldman Sachs, Gaddafi, Mubarak, Saddam Hussein, and bin Laden, to name just a few. Anyone can become a pawn to be used, supported, and then despised or eliminated, depending upon the needs of imperial expansion and global hegemony.

The latest instantiation of trouble in our increasingly troubling imperialistic drive was betrayed by recent events and commentary surrounding the apparent assassination of Osama bin Laden, America's latest version of the incarnate face of Evil! And the talking points have been reiterated non-stop by media idiots and other paid counter-conspiracy theory pundits.

The fact is that we were beside-ourselves with joy to support the master terrorist when he was fighting the Evil Empire, as those Soviet Commies were attempting to "liberate" Afghanistan from the unwashed Islamic hordes. With prodding from our CIA, we supplied Osama and his "freedom fighters" with the know-how and weaponry to stave off the unholy aggressors and defend their homeland. We used him as a puppet in our Cold War battle against the great Soviet Bear. He was our fair-haired Muslim boy, our bearded savior from the holy land. But then, when our own creeping assault upon the sacred soil became more clearly manifest, defiling and despoiling the sacred spaces as we moved – from Kuwait and Iraq to Yemen, Saudi Arabia, and now Libya – bin Laden quickly recognized that Uncle Sam and our hegemonic designs were the real threat to his holy land, to their religious and cultural traditions, as we sought to gain control of their liquid gold, the OIL that maintains our unsustainable and deluded, infidel lifestyle.

But the USA also needed a reason to increase its incursions into MENA, so perhaps the CIA was tapped again to call upon its old friend Osama to wreak some havoc on our own soils (9/11), and get the American populace behind a larger war of occupation and control in the Middle East and the Arabian Peninsula. Given the history of our covert operations, deceptions and machinations (as Wikileaks has clearly demonstrated), it is not entirely out of the question. Perhaps this is why conspiracy theories still run rampant; and why this Administration (in the person of Dr. 'Sunny' Sunstein) wants to squelch them pronto. And perhaps that is why we finally had to pop Osama - "Geronimo" – quickly and quietly, without trial or public discussion, because the wholly/holy Evil One knew too much.

With our relentless assaults in that region and the rest of the globe, we continue to increase our military budgets exponentially for imperial expansion and the goodies it promises to deliver – oil, markets, and slave-wage labor. All the while taking our own social programs to the killing floor of the abattoir, seeking to disembowel senior citizens and the poor, and perhaps then, the middle class. (Katie, bar the doors!!)

So what is happening here? Well, disenfranchised socialists, libertarians and communists all smell blood in the water. Yet the larger body politic – the proletariat or petite bourgeoisie (depending upon your perspective) – is not so quick to jump on any of these tired bandwagons. In fact, many among the masses are exploring alternative solutions concerning the trajectory and velocity of change necessary to avert the direst of outcomes. And among them are voices loosely crying for a retreat or even the termination of the executioner... death to the State and its alien authority.

These calls come from the would-be anarchists of today... not because they want chaos to reign; rather, because they feel the archaic pull of a more primal autonomy, some feral memory trace that was lost with the establishment of kingdoms, nations, empires, legislators, and other anonymous, impersonal hierarchies.

Yes, a revolution seems imminent. But it does not promise to be soft or unifying; rather, it looks to be one of disintegration. And while the secessionist movements may have gained serious momentum among certain left-leaning elements during the second coming of the Burning Bush era, this revolution may not be led by liberals or progressives, but rather by conservatives and independents, perhaps by the slap-happy-gun-tottin'-Tea-partiers themselves; those who prefer limited federal authority and minimal government in general. And now, the GOP (a.k.a. Sister Sarah) is looking to create further divisions within the USA over the "Osama Kill."

But when the divisiveness escalates, and fists (err... bullets) start to fly, with a few States perhaps attempting secession from the Union, these new anarchists may begin to make their own moves, taking advantage of the vulnerability of both the Union and the States.

As heir-apparent of Western progress with constantly expanding hierarchies of social, political, and economic complexity, the self-described beacon of hope to the rest of humanity, this American landscape is now a fitting body-politic for a complete reversal of course; the rejection of hierarchy, of legislative control, and the complexity of the civilized state. It appears increasingly to be the unlikely harbinger of the recovery of a more primal, instinctual freedom. (What did Freud call it, "the return of the repressed?")

America is a land ripe for cultural, economic and political disintegration in the interests of recovering some lost simplicity. All hinges upon the nature, dynamics and momentum of the revolutionary spirit, and to what extent it can overcome the inertia of standing cultural and political hegemonic forces. But the fairytales we tell ourselves, and the myths we have come to believe in, simply to maintain this ignorance and our loyalty to this dream-turned-nightmare, carry too great a price for even people like Sarah-know-nothing or Joe-nobody to put up with and stay their hand much longer.

Will the coming end of the American empire have us running in retreat from a world populated by the likes of Mad Max, a war of all against all? Or will it be the highly anticipated coming of the Kingdom of God on earth? Neither I think! If revolutionary forces succeed in mobilizing this passion for disintegration, and if such passion can fuel the anarchist's vision for community without authority, without a head of state, then perhaps this hegemony can be dismantled and "we, the people," can rediscover a renewed form of community — real communities built upon simple respect for the other (including the earth), an appreciation of self-sufficiency born of cooperation, and an expansive sense of kinship – both consanguinal and affine relations. But let's not hope for it; there's already been too much of that "hopey" thing lately.

*****

An Exercise in Cross Cultural Phenomenology

On Ordinariness: A View from the Steppe

> *By virtue of natality and the ability to act, each new individual poses a threat to civilization. The child carries barbarism with him or her.* [Einer Overenget, *Hannah Arendt*]

Let's begin with an agreement. Civilization is, in part, about making distinctions; how those distinctions are drawn – what is foreground, what background, and what remains unnamed – provides each culture its unique view of the world. Language, and of course writing, is a vital accomplice in this activity that "cuts" the world up into so many pieces, creating typical perspectives, customs and beliefs, patterns of perception and manipulation. In short, it seeks to define order where formerly there was just (dare we say it) ordinary stuff. The underlying logic of each language will determine in large measure how these distinctions are drawn and what categories are applicable within different cultural contexts or horizons. At the same time, however, the physical environment – the specificity of geography, climate, etc. – will have some impact on the content of the categories developed within different native tongues.

But what about this "barbarism" Øverenget refers to above in his reading of Hannah Arendt? Is it really true that civilization must fight continuously to maintain its delicate conceptual hold on reality, to keep the weeds from overtaking the paved highways, so to speak? Can it be that each new human life poses such a threat to the well-ordered world we have built? Is there really a question of these little "barbarians" doing additional malice to an environment already cut-up and divided into so many pieces by the predominant culture?

Perhaps the real challenge is that the mere appearance of these newcomers suggests the possibility of an incipient erasure or "healing" of those cultural cuts, signaling a return to a more amorphous state of affairs in which we all found ourselves initially thrown. As Rousseau has suggested, the principal function of a civil society is the sublimation of the natural man (read barbarian) in order to recreate him or her with a new nature. In *The Social Contract* (II, 7), he writes,

> *[The Legislator must] so to speak change human nature, transform each individual, who by himself is a perfect and solitary whole, into part of a greater whole from which that individual as it were gets his life and his being; weaken man's constitution to strengthen it; substitute a partial and moral existence for the physical and independent existence which we all have received from nature. He must, in a word, take man's own forces away from him in order to give him forces which are foreign to him and which he cannot use without the help of others. The more the natural forces are dead and annihilated the greater and more lasting the acquired ones...*

So here's the story: while our pre-civilized ancestors were transformed through some act of existential surgery (or perhaps butchery) thereby becoming citizens of the State — so that we now see ourselves and the world in terms of distinctions provided by the institutionalized categories of civilized life — the incidence of yet unacculturated/undomesticated infants in our midst may yet remind us of that paradise lost and threaten a fall back into some indeterminate, more primitive mode of being.

But not only did civil society remake each individual into a proper citizen; in the process it also remade the surrounding everyday environment into an apparently well-managed world, a cosmos. Furthermore, there is a tendency in such culture-building activity not simply to maintain but also to expand the orderliness, to eradicate any possible arbitrariness or wildness that might threaten to dissolve the boundaries and betray the underlying condition of a more primitive grounding.

But how to account for this imposition of civilization's artifice on top of that more unassuming, inchoate ground that preceded it, which might again arbitrarily impinge upon the more recently crafted spectacle of civic life?

We continue briefly with this myth of origins. As Hobbes and Locke have maintained in slightly different formulations, the pre-civilized state of nature can be rather arbitrary and unpredictable, and at times a dangerously ill suited place to satisfy even humankind's most basic need for food and shelter. So, it becomes the chief mission of civil society to establish clearly articulated boundaries in which it is safe for all members to pursue their lives together harmoniously, rationally, and without fear. Through the benefits of inter-subjective agreement (now made practicable by written language), the institutions of civil society create rational frameworks for the commonwealth, establishing structure and an order within which people are required to conform to clearly articulated norms.

But this new world, as Rousseau suggests, is anything but natural; rather, it is pure artifice, a *politic* construction of new forces allowing citizens to work and live together safely within a well-defined universe. But, lost beneath the categorical neatness of such cultural contrivance, life's fundamentally arbitrary and unstructured wildness recedes from view while still lurking just under the surface, challenging civilization's very ability to establish, maintain, and control its well-ordered cosmos.

As colorful as these philosophical reflections might seem, we must shift our focus momentarily to explore such characterizations in terms of a more readily accessible transition from pre-urban, pre-literate settlements of kinship-based groupings, into our more stratified urban societies. In his succinct manner, Marvin Bram characterizes the two hundred thousand year period of human pre-history – before the birth of modern civilized states – as the "kinship era" after its form of social organization. As he defines it:

Kinship means that what urban peoples call political, social, economic, and cultural arrangements are made not by specialists or professionals, usually strangers to most persons, but by the elders of clans, well known to all clans persons.

The "post-kinship era," on the other hand, is characterized by the growth of cities and the development of writing, with precisely those forms of impersonal hierarchical institutions that we currently find operating in the modern State today; and according to most accounts, this transition occurred approximately fifty-five hundred years ago in the Middle East and Central Asian Steppe.

Embracing kindred observations by Alexis de Tocqueville in his commentary on nineteenth-century America, Bram writes,

[In a 'post-kinship' era] the nuclear family by itself cannot resist the impingements of modern political and economic institutions: the father, mother, and their children must be surrounded by some intermediate, protective body of persons in order to be safe from unacceptable levels of control. In fact, those modern political and economic institutions could not have been created in the first place unless the original protective body of persons, the clan, was broken into its constituent and susceptible parts, its nuclear families. The first emergence of civilization in the Middle East, and all subsequent civilized nations, were constructed on the break-up of their pre-urban clans. (Recovery of the West, 2002)

This sounds not unlike Rousseau's presumption about the replacement of man's "natural forces" with new "foreign forces," without which one cannot survive in civil society. We can surmise then that with the birth of civilized societies (documented by the written word) there was a momentous transformation in how human beings began to relate both to one another and to the world around them, and that whatever was lost in this transition haunts humanity even today.

How might we explore this underlying and arbitrary wildness haunting our common culture, threatening to encroach upon and otherwise disrupt the safe haven of civilized existence? In "Transculture and Society," post-Soviet émigré Mikhail Epstein gets very close to capturing its essence with his concept of "the ordinary."

The ordinary can be defined as something indefinable that exits in the gap, in the pause, in between cultural categories. (Transcultural Experiments, 1999)

Now, most modern civilized States seek to account for every extension of space and every moment in time, every potential variable, so that no "gaps" appear to exist within the fabric of its complex civic or psychic life; no semiotic vagueness remains that could lead citizens into confusion or indecision. Let us call such cultures *tightly woven*. Much effort may be expended on this objective alone; reclaim, delete or eliminate any marginal, indeterminate, or arbitrary influences – build out and polish every centimeter of the natural world, close the borders, assimilate the culturally aberrant, and bring everyone and everything into the big tent – in an effort to insure the sanctity and security of the grand spectacle.

My initial wager is that this vague (albeit often arresting) sense of life's *ordinariness* embodies a real limit-experience in the tight weave of our cultural formatting. It is disorienting because it pushes at the edge of commonly shared expectations – temporally, spatially and psychically. It may reveal itself in the most mundane of circumstances, where one simply loses control in an otherwise apparently well managed life, or where a purely unanticipated event occurs in an otherwise functional society; for example, when you awake in the morning to prepare for work only to find there is no hot water coming from your tap, or when the heat suddenly goes off in the wee hours of the night while the temperature outside is well-below freezing. In other words, it may be something that quite arbitrarily shakes us out of this carefully constructed artifice and brings us again face to face with our own irreducible, inescapable sentience – our own raw presence in the world.

If this feeling of *ordinariness* appears in the gaps of our cultural fabric, perhaps we can better recognize it by pursuing a cross-cultural perspective. After spending a number of years in Western Siberia on the Euro-Asian Steppe, in and around the reasonably sized city of Barnaul, there is a strange feeling of existential displacement here that is quite unlike anything I have felt before, even in other parts of Europe. On the one hand, Russians are notorious for their toleration of bureaucratic neatness and institutional hierarchies, directing and organizing every aspect of civic life. Yet, there is an extra-cultural innocence here that hearkens back to a simpler world... one that takes me back to a time over fifty years ago when I was a child growing-up in America.

The year was 1958 and I can still recall walking to the end of the street from our home in a small town thirty miles outside of New York City; from there, I could follow various meandering paths into the woods made by the frequent comings and goings of us kids as we explored a natural wasteland just at the edge of town that spilled over into our small community. It was an unused, but not pristine forested area – a wild, undeveloped territory apparently belonging to no one. And there were numerous unmarked, but well-wrought shortcuts through this forest and field that led to other small communities, shops, or sledding areas that we so loved on wintry days. For years this place went officially unrecognized by our community (except to us little barbarians); but it was not accorded the privilege of remaining undeveloped. After several years it was annexed and became part of a local urban development plan. But while we children enjoyed ourselves there, this place was unstructured and unaffected; it was what I would describe now as a place of artlessness and spontaneity, an undefined intersection of our domesticated world, an occurrence of the *ordinary* without signs or cultural safeguards. And it is precisely such experiences that you still find so frequently in the great Siberian Steppe today, where, as Epstein remarks,

The insufficiency of mapping, of cultural demarcations, makes life more dangerous and uncomfortable than it is in the West. You do not know where you are, on the edge of a forest or on the site of a future building: nature is polluted and culture is diffused. But this is what creates ordinariness. (TE)

On a recent summer day in Barnaul my wife Anna decided to take us for a stroll. Walking down the broken pavement drive from our apartment block, she led me off the main road and across a rather overgrown and untended field at the far-end of which was a deep cropping of birch trees. As we wandered into this unused parcel of land, there was a dirt footpath haphazardly winding through the tall grass leading indirectly to the out-cropping of trees. We followed that path into the trees, at which point we entered a wooded area interspersed with some discarded evidences of civilization, where we could hear sounds of unrest - both animals and children playing in the trees. Emerging on the other side of this wood, we found ourselves at a clearing with several shops positioned before us.

Obviously, this was a well-worn path through a wild, ill-defined parcel of land, connecting two different communities. It was not the planned way of getting from here to there, articulated neither by roads, curbs nor street signs; but it was a way that many local feet had trodden, perhaps hurriedly at times on colder winter days; and it perfectly reflected how this feeling of *ordinariness* can penetrate everyday life here.

My first impression of this and similar incidents was that Siberia was simply less developed than I was accustomed to in America; and that was certainly true. But this preliminary assessment did not quite capture what I was experiencing here; and furthermore, it begged the question of why there was a preponderance of such gaps within the cultural infrastructure — spatially, temporally and psychically. It seemed to me that there was more going on here, but because it was so unfamiliar to me conceptually it was not until I accidentally happened upon Epstein's own analyses and his comparison with what he found in America that I was able to grasp this indeterminacy somewhat more clearly.

[In Russia] when you go through a meadow you always find several narrow paths that were not designed by the developers of this territory but spontaneously created by people who need to make a shortcut from one village to another. While walking these paths you feel the blessed meaning of the ordinary that does not belong to any category, which spontaneously emerges and remains arbitrary...(TE)

This seemed to describe more adequately what I was experiencing. There was a palpable unpredictability and carefreeness not only on such meandering paths but elsewhere in daily life, betraying an almost feral freedom from the structuring machinations of civilization, a source of spontaneity lodged somewhere within the far recesses of my body, and most certainly within the Russian experience. And somehow this feeling touched me physically and psychologically to my core.

As I came to recognize, the quality of my own feelings in these situations was reflected as well in the way such occasions were met with, accepted and even relished by the local populations; not just by children, but by people of all ages, income levels, educational, and professional backgrounds. No one was exempt from wandering these back paths and recognizing the quiet whimsical feeling that they evoked. And, as people here point out, there is an abundance of space and time in Russia, enough space and time to walk even without a specific destination in view. In the Russian language there is a term to denote such "aimless walking around," *gulyat*, which clearly connotes that such activity has no definitive purpose or objective – just walking.

This same attitude is observed, as well, in how Siberians deal with other rather fluid moments or circumstances in life: for example, spending time at a modest *dacha* or country cottage resting, fishing or hand-cultivating a small plot of land; spending time in the vast Siberian forests foraging for berries or mushrooms; or even resting at a primitive *banya* (wood-fired steam room) just relaxing with friends or family. In each instance one gets the unspoken message that now we will enjoy a cultural "time-out," a break from the recognized orderliness and noise of a routinely civilized existence. Even that term *gulyat* (just walking) has a more colloquial meaning – "to have a day off from work," "to make merry," or "to live it up." Again, this betrays an affinity in the Russian experience between a primal physical meandering and the psychic spaciousness of a more relaxed, less-structured existence. And if you ask anyone about this fluidity, about the apparent abundance of gaps in the ordering of life here, they will tell you that it makes life more interesting. Indeed, they will tell you how difficult it is to make plans in Siberia because life may suddenly – spontaneously, arbitrarily – intervene and disrupt your plans. Perhaps what we have here is a more loosely woven cultural fabric, dictated in part by the specific gravity of the Russian soul.

Suffice it to say that such experiences cannot be forced into simple categorical dichotomies like nature versus culture, or disorder versus order; such categorizations might lead to misunderstanding the lived-experience here. Rather these incidences are ordinary in the sense of remaining artless or capricious, if you will, arbitrary; disclosed in the subtle dissolution of hard conceptual distinctions, in that gap where the normal chatter of civilization is broken by a preeminent silence.

Let me recount another brief example from the Steppe – a trip to Lake Balkhash in the former Soviet Republic of Kazakhstan from the small town of Tekeli. This was an adventure in uncle Volodya's car, with one of his friends following closely behind. The two-hour drive down old patched roads to a turn-off at an unmarked dirt intersection led our small entourage into a crisscrossing set of paths through massive sand dunes, slowly leading us further into an untamed-looking desert area. There were no signs, no concrete byways, no parking areas, and no vendors selling towels, souvenirs or frosty cones; there was just unmarked dune after dune, with an occasional broken down vehicle along the path that evidently could not finish its journey.

At the end of this drive, with many false starts and wrong turns – like on the back of a two humped camel – we arrived at the edge of an enormous lake; again no signs, no demarcation, no designated parking areas. Several more spins around the last dune left our two cars vying for position close to the water, but parallel to each other so that we could make camp by throwing a tarp over the two cars and creating a shelter in between them. Again, for me this was just such an irreducible experience of life's *ordinariness*, of my bare facticity in the world, breaking-through a rather large gap in the fabric...

And as Epstein suggests, such occurrences are all but absent in the American experience today, where

> *Even islands of spontaneity such as natural parks and preserves are carefully demarcated; their very naturalness is the object of cultivation... so that even nature is reduced to the sign of nature ("wildlife refuge")... In American national parks or wilderness areas the boundary between culture and nature is drawn very strictly with exactitude of several centimeters. There are special trails that delineate the route of penetration of culture into the domain of nature. But neither cultural nor natural areas in themselves create the feeling of ordinariness. (TE)*

Having lived the bulk of my life in America, including twenty-years in

Colorado ("Where The West Still Lives"), I can verify his assessment; our approach to naturalness (the spontaneous, the wild, the arbitrary) is to cultivate it – map it out, clean it up and deodorize it – so that it becomes part of the plan; an easily accessible piece of "Nature" that everyone can enjoy while still comfortably ensconced within a seamlessly civilized world.

Now, what makes the Russian vantage point so compelling here is the archeological and paleontological evidence suggesting that the Altai Region of Siberia represents perhaps one of the most primitive and independent origins of human habitation tens, if not hundreds of thousands of years ago; the location of some of the earliest kinship groupings known to modern research. So as we reflect on the birth of civilization (and myths of origin) we might imagine that the prehistoric incidence of simple "band egalitarian societies" in the Altai Mountains of Russia could represent one of the factical locations of those very transformations of our pre-urban ancestors into post-kinship citizens – with the attendant sublimation of a more primal experience of human dwelling that underlies and haunts our civilization today. And it might even be argued that throughout Russia's long and arduous history one can see an unrelenting affection for this obscured aspect of our common humanity, as demonstrated by the continued inherence and influence on the Russian psyche of the simple and perhaps uncivilizable, but well-mythologized, peasant soul.

Moreover, the severity and vastness of this great Siberian terrain militates against a comprehensive ordering of the natural world, encouraging such spontaneity and providing ample opportunity for the chance emergence of *ordinariness* within the world-as-lived.

In Russia there are huge semi-developed territories where culture and nature are so confused and diffused in each other that one feels this inordinate place is the true place of the ordinary. (TE)

One final, but not insignificant example is a typical Russian experience of waiting in endless queues — at the bank, the train station, the phone company, or the local housing registration office. These queues seem to appear spontaneously because as you enter a room people are not necessarily lined-up, one directly behind another; rather they may just be sitting haphazardly around, meandering about the room, or outside having a smoke. So you must inquire as to who is last in line, even though no queue visibly exists; yet everyone seems to know his or her place. Milling around, just waiting: "you can feel life...so slow and empty that reality reveals its authentic substance and duration." *(TE)*

As Epstein concludes, "what makes the ordinary so precious is *the spontaneity* of human actions, the growth of the natural out of the cultural." *(TE)* And this is perhaps what the above reading of Hannah Arendt may be suggesting; that each yet-un-enculturated little person bears within him or herself an "excess of existence that does not fit into any existing cultural model" and cannot be easily assimilated into the civilized milieu – a surplus of just being, which her very presence can bring crashing down upon us at any moment, thereby disrupting our otherwise secure cosmos.

So how are we to make sense of this experience of *ordinariness* if there is really no easy way to grasp it in terms of our shared cultural categories? Is it like knowing we are in the presence of the Sacred, which according to most religious traditions cannot be described adequately in everyday language? Perhaps there is something embedded deep within human nature, and in the nature of the symbolic systems we create, that always presents us with the possibility of recovering this experience within (or out of) the cultural, anywhere at anytime.

But, what could this be? Well, perhaps it is not so mysterious after all. If the artifice of civilization creates our basic orientation in reality, with conceptual prejudices to protect us from oblique experiences of extra-cultural apparitions, then surely there are certain limit situations where this feeling might burst through unabated. Obviously, these would most likely be culturally confusing circumstances where our normal conceptual frameworks come into question or simply do not function properly, conditions that breed cultural ambiguity.

But whether the specific cause of such ambiguity be rooted in more personally unsettling moments of loneliness, anguish, suffering, madness and boredom, or perhaps born of more shared experiences of disruption, like foreign travel, emigration, cross-cultural exchange, or more dramatically perhaps, threats of terrorism, a consistent element in all these limit situations is the sudden or even subtle experience of marginality or strangeness: an incipient feeling of difference, otherness or Alterity, either in the sense of being-beside oneself, coping with the Alterity of a strange world or a stranger in our midst, or even an emergent awareness of the otherness of our own cultural landscape.

Let us briefly gloss two views of the stranger in sociological theory, to highlight both the interior and exterior faces of such otherness.

The stranger, like the poor and sundry 'inner enemies,' is an element of the group itself. His position as a full-fledged member involves both being outside it and confronting it... (The Sociology of Georg Simmel)

The cultural pattern of the approached group is to the stranger not a shelter but a field of adventure, not a matter of course but a questionable topic of investigation... (Alfred Schutz, *Collected Papers, II*)

And, while we are all strangers to ourselves because we are artful products of civilized reconstruction, we are also strangers to our culture "because we come to a given society from our childhood [read barbarism], from our loneliness, from those extra-cultural and countercultural niches that are common to the majority of people all over the world." *(TE)*

For the stranger then, either within or outside of us, the normal categories of the group become marginalized and problematic. It is in this respect that otherness and strangeness become likely protagonists in the experience of the *ordinary*; unpredictable, these are culturally marginal elements haunting each individual, making each of us aware of our own mundane humanity, our own facticity. In this respect, the outsider in our midst or the stranger within positions us face to face with a vision of what we are not, but what we might have been...our own potentiality for being other than we are or never having been at all, in other words, the possibility of our own non-being.

Whenever we are confronted by such marginality or have the feeling of being adrift without the safety and security of our cultural world (psychically, semiotically or physically), it is precisely in these gaps that we may be struck by the *ordinariness* of life. And this experience uniquely possesses the capacity to expose both the artlessness and arbitrariness of our own existence, because it is in the face of this marginality – where we rub up against the limits of normal cultural controls – that we are most apt to recognize the accidental nature of our own culturally defined world, and so become dumbstruck by life's simple extension and duration.

Perhaps wherever individuals come face to face with their own facticity, the raw embodiment and presence of simply being in the world, demonstrating a "bare courage and patience to be," perhaps this is what it means to experience life's *ordinariness*, offering us but a glimpse of that capriciousness, that unfiltered barbarism, always lying beneath the surface of each enculturated citizen, as a potential event and a haunting reminder of both our forgotten origins and our pending demise!

And perhaps this is why the barbarian in our midst or within poses such a threat to civilization, because a citizenry so exposed would be very difficult to control indeed!

*****

www.ingramcontent.com/pod-product-compliance
Lightning Source LLC
Chambersburg PA
CBHW021039160726
47994CB00006B/2630